Acclaim for *The Whole Youth Worker*

"If you are a youth worker who struggles with staying in ministry for one reason or another, reading this book will remind you that you are not alone. As you read about Jay's experiences you will see some frustration and hurt associated with the daily task of being a youth worker. If you want to hear from the heart of a youth worker who struggles to enjoy the Monday to Friday part of youth ministry and wants to help you get through it too, then you need to read *The Whole Youth Worker.*"

—Mike Kupferer, *Youth Ministry Exchange*

"Don't let anyone fool you—youth ministry is harder than it looks! In *The Whole Youth Worker*, Jay gives us a glimpse at what it's like to be in the trenches—both good and bad. You will read this book and say, 'Been there—it's good to know I'm not alone!'"

—Rev. Bill Fisackerly, IV,
Gulf Cove United Methodist Church

"*The Whole Youth Worker* will help guide most youth workers around the dangerous curves and out of the sinkholes of youth ministry. This short, 148-page, readable paperback, has very valuable, sensible, workable counsel that most every person who works with teenagers in an ecclesiastical setting ought to read. If you're a Senior Pastor wondering what to give your Youth Minister to help them negotiate this important work, then this is the book to get"

—Rev. Michael Philliber, PhD, *ReaderViews*

"Jay Tucker does a fantastic job giving practical advice to all youth workers. The joy and passion he holds for his career reach out and grab your attention. His fresh approach and great sense of humor will help inspire and renew your outlook on the world of youth ministry. I plan on keeping this book close at hand for years to come and I will be sharing it with many people."

—Daniel Wilde (Nashville, TN)

"Here is a brass-tacks companion for those who would aspire to being not a master but a servant, one who is willing to put forth great effort on the young, even though not all the recipients will be appreciative. Jay Tucker is the opposite of preachy. He is practical and instructional with down-to-earth language that brings a smile.

I feel that I have met this man in person and benefitted greatly by the experience. He is the genuine article, with the heart of a servant but the mind of a teacher. He knows what kids are like these days, and he loves them anyway."

Rev. Heyward B. Ewart,III PhD,
author of *AM I BAD? Recovering From Abuse*

"Jay's book is simple, straightforward and real. if you are a parent who is going to put your children into a youth group, read it. If you are a pastor looking for a youth leader, read it. I can tell you I know what I need to look for when it comes time for my children to spend time in a youth group."

Jeff Murray, Melbourne FL

the WHOLE YOUTH WORKER

Advice On Professional, Personal, and Physical Wellness from the Trenches

2nd Edition

By Jay Tucker

Foreword by Jeanne Mayo

Loving Healing Press

2011

Back cover photo by Angela Sackett of Loving Legacy Photography (Tampa Bay, FL).

Library of Congress Cataloging-in-Publication Data

Tucker, Jason, 1973-
  The whole youth worker : advice on professional, personal, and physical wellness from the trenches / Jay Tucker ; foreword by Jeanne Mayo. -- 2nd ed.
      p. cm.
  Includes bibliographical references and index.
  ISBN-13: 978-1-61599-078-8 (pbk. : alk. paper)
  ISBN-10: 1-61599-078-X (pbk. : alk. paper)
  ISBN-13: 978-1-61599-041-2 (hardcover : alk. paper)
  ISBN-10: 1-61599-041-0 (hardcover : alk. paper)
  1. Church work with youth. I. Title.
  BV4447.T83 2011
  259'.23--dc22
                                        2011000030

Distributed by: Ingram Book Group, New Leaf Distributing, Quality Books.

Published by:
Loving Healing Press
5145 Pontiac Trail
Ann Arbor, MI 48105-9627

Email info@LHPress.com
Web www.LovingHealing.com
Tollfree 888-761-6268
Fax 734-663-6861

Contents

Acknowledgments

This book is dedicated with love and many thank-yous to:

My Lord Jesus Christ who is the author of this crazy yet amazing life I live

My Godly, gorgeous, and amazing wife Kimberly who deserves 99% of the credit for the good stuff I do in life. I love you.

My children Sarah Kay and William Monroe II, you are Daddy's greatest gifts.

The memory of my parents William and Sandra Tucker.

Dale and Lura Hannula, for your Godly example and love.

Ken and Vanessa Sackett, for your Godly example and love.

Brian, Angela, Brian Jr., Joshua, Anna, Ethan, and Isaac Sackett, the best example of what a Godly family should be.

Rev. Jerry, Nancy, Lindsey, and Erin Gardner, our friends forever...I can't thank you enough.

Rev. Richard Nussel, thank you for taking a chance on a guy with zero experience.

Neil and Claudia Cook, thank you for your friendship, love, and never ending prayer.

Rev. William, Kim, Bethany, Ally, and Wil Fisackerly...You guys are family.

Wade Stockman, you inspire me everyday...*not one step* buddy!

Pastors Walter Fohs and Becky Robbins-Penniman, you both are inspiring to work with.

And to every student I've ever had and ever will have in youth ministry. You are the reasons I do what I do!

Preface to the 2nd Edition

One of the highlights of my life was when my first book, *The Whole Youth Worker*, was published two years ago. The book came out while a very dark time in my life was beginning. I was adjusting to the first extended period of time in my life without a job since the age of fifteen. It wasn't easy to adjust to not being needed. At first, I looked at my situation as the opportunity to spend some quality time with my son. After seven months, I was ready to hurt the persons responsible for the creation of *Spongebob Squarepants*. I was more than ready to go back to work.

That opportunity came in August 2009, when I accepted a job at Nicaea Academy to teach at a small private Christian school. I was hired as a "high school" teacher which meant I was teaching six different subjects a day. Having a degree in elementary education, the idea of teaching several different subjects in a day wasn't a foreign concept. However, there is a difference in preparing for 6 lessons on the elementary level. I typically have those skills mastered! High school was a different story. I was teaching complicated subjects that I hadn't given any thought to in twenty years. *Did I really want to feed my family so bad?*

I wouldn't trade my time at Nicaea for anything. There I spent my days with some of the most amazing young people and dedicated teachers I have ever worked with. I definitely had some characters! The irreverent teenage "Sweat Hogs" from that 1970s show *Welcome Back, Kotter* had nothing on the great group of kids that I had the honor to teach on a daily basis. I have to mention one student in my class because he was a challenging kid whom you couldn't help but love. In addition, he has the most made-for-action-movies name I've ever heard: Dare Rambo will rule the world one day.

I got a phone call around Christmas time from a great church in my town that was looking for a youth minister. After much prayer and discussion with my wife, I was reminded that youth ministry is my life's calling. I accepted the opportunity to be interviewed and was eventually honored with the position. As I write this, I am finishing up my first year at the church. I almost forgot mentioning how much I love working in the church.

That isn't to say that my present church isn't without its own set of challenges. All churches are! My current youth group consists of roughly thirty-five 5th through 12th grade students. The majority of these students are middle=school girls, a challenge that reminds me daily of the importance of prayer. I find my current position as proof positive that God has a great sense of humor.

These past two years have made me a more organized and appreciative youth worker. I wake up every morning at 6:45am to take my kids to school and return home to get ready for a new day in youth ministry. Our God is truly an awesome God!

This 2nd edition contains five new chapters and a collection of new stories that I pray will make you think, laugh, and embrace God a little more tightly.

Foreword

I'm writing this Foreword amidst the animated chatter of my family right after our holiday celebration. And though it's years after my child-rearing season, I remain eternally grateful that my primary ministry didn't begin when I drove out of the Mayo driveway, but rather, when I drove back in.

Now, over four exciting decades into the youth ministry journey, I am reveling in the endless rewards of living a Christ-centered, balanced life. Our sons both love Jesus and love us—in an indisputable and life-giving way. They both are passionately in fulltime ministry and managed to avoid the "I want to follow the Antichrist" phase during their growing up years. Their father remains my treasured "boyfriend" and the ultimate earthly hero in life. We just celebrated our 40th anniversary together at a "Vow Renewal Ceremony" that my amazing ministry team surprised us with last month. And to make my journey even more utopian, I'm now "Nana" to the two cutest grandsons in the known universe!

The precious gifts of my life are even more treasured today because of a phone conversation I had only moments ago. As I write this foreword, my mind is racing with the starkness of the contrast. You see, tonight a veteran youth pastor is announcing to his students that he is resigning his position due to "moral indiscretions." He leaves straight from his youth service for the airport. His flight takes him to another state where his new-found "soulmate" awaits. My attempts an hour ago to change his direction seemed to be pretty fruitless. He leaves young children in the wake of his selfishness... and a shattered, confused group of teenagers at his church.

That's why Jay Tucker's book, "The Whole Youth Worker," is such an authentic gift to youth pastors and workers. It calls us to wholeness in all arenas of our life. You see, you can "cram" for earthly exams; but you can't cram for most character ones. True tests of character usually come as "pop quizzes." So it's only through living a balanced, healthy life—spiritually, family-wise, emotionally and physically—that we can thrive long haul amidst the pressures of "doing youth ministry" while also "doing life."

As a love note to youth workers who will read these words, I'd like to pass on some simple mentoring/ coaching thoughts from my vantage point of four decades in the trenches. Let me highlight a few things that you will hear echoed throughout Jay's book:

Decide what you will give to the world: A gifted man in youth ministry who is *outwardly empowered*...or a broken man in youth ministry who is *inwardly transformed*. There is a world of difference, you know. Wise leaders always choose the latter. I've watched countless youth ministry superstars "crash and burn" because charisma became a suitable substitute for character.

Remember that you'll rarely notice changes in your own spiritual life or character, no matter how sincere you are. Why? Those strategic changes *sneak up on you quietly* like weight gain—one tiny bit at a time. So be brutally honest with your own compromises, motivations, and sin. Living a Christ-honoring life isn't glamorous or media-worthy. But it's still the only thing that is celebrated in eternity.

Make a "daily appointment time" with the Lord and actually *have* a consistent devotional life instead of just preaching about it. Consistency always trumps length. So start with a daily "10 and 10" (10 minutes in the Word and 10 minutes in prayer) and build from there. I've never counseled a moral failure in the ministry who had even a relatively consistent devotional life—*never.*

Fight fiercely the voices in your head that will haunt you with your own failures and tell you how unworthy and fruitless you are in youth ministry. The enemy's main battleground for you will always in the privacy of your mind. Only you can keep choosing to "bring your thoughts into captivity."

"How long will the mind games last?" you ask me. Well, they're still alive and well at the 40-year-mark in my ministry. Sorry about my discouraging truthfulness. But I've learned to focus on only what I want to fuel. Mental discipline becomes easier as the years roll by.

If you have children, realize that they must never compete with your youth ministry. The title bestowed on the most important leader in the world today is not president, Olympic medalist, or pastor. It is *parent.* Our children are the *living messages* we send forward into a time we will probably never see. Long after ministry is a dim memory, your family will still be with you. So steward those relationships with great care. The enemy will always attempt to make the people who are the most *precious* in your life to feel the most *common.*

Prioritize *people* over *pulpits.* your youth messages will be forgotten with agonizing speed. But the teenagers in your ministry will never forget *how the Jesus inside of you made them feel.* And just remember: If you're out of the "people business," you're really out of authentic youth ministry.

Thank God every day of your life that you *get* to do youth ministry! Studies tell us that 92% of all decisions for Christ are made on or before one's 18th birthday. That places huge destiny on what we are investing our lives into. People will rarely celebrate you and teenagers won't sing you choruses of "How Great Thou Art." But we have a purpose that is both true and eternal. Jim Elliott said it powerfully: "He is no fool who gives what he cannot keep... to gain what he cannot lose."

Remember that the only things that walk back from the cemetery with the mourners and *refuse to be buried* are the character of the man and his spiritual fruit. So live with the end in mind; and make Hell regret you ever decided to love some teenagers.

D.L. Moody is one of my favorites in the Christian Hall of Fame. Near his death, he said something that I've chosen as one of my own personal mantras:

> "When I die, don't think I'm gone. I'll still
> be alive in that person... and that person...
> and that person."

So as you read *The Whole Youth Worker* by Jay Tucker, realize that you have chosen one of the most Christ-honoring endeavors in the universe—that of multiplying your heart for Christ into teenagers and college students in the 21st century. May you do it with such integrity and passion that your "that-person-line" will reach to the stars and back!

> Lovingly Cheering For You, Jeanne Mayo
> President, Youth Leader's Coach
> Youth Pastor, Author, and Speaker

PART I

Working with Youth

He replied, "Because you have so little faith. I tell you the truth, if you have faith as small as a mustard seed, you can say to this mountain, 'Move from here to there' and it will move. Nothing will be impossible for you."

Matthew 17:20 (*NIV*)

1 Hey Youth Minister, You Rock!

Ten years. That's two tours of duty, more than two Presidential terms, and long enough to get an advanced degree. I've been in full-time youth ministry for eight years. Some of you who might be reading this have put in eight years in just lock-ins alone. (I have nothing but respect, love, and admiration for you nuts that have been doing this for a decade or more.) So I am, by no means, the expert when it comes to youth ministry. All I can tell you is my journey and how I've managed to last a decade.

When I look at the statistics for youth ministry, I see that I am one of a dying breed. Lots of young men and women are getting into youth ministry, and then right back out. The main reasons seem to be stress, poor pay and little benefits, and the realization that you can't just play videogames all day and you won't ever be called "The coolest guy in the world." This is tough work. You have my permission to punch the next person right in the nose who asks, "When are you going to become a real pastor?" (Just kidding, that is hardly ever a good idea.)

Maybe some of you are currently volunteering as a youth minister, Sunday School teacher, youth rep on your church board, or the extra pair of hands. First of all, thank you. Without you, most of the ministry wouldn't get done. Now that I've said thank you, let me say something that might offend you a little. You probably don't completely understand what it's like to be the Y.M.I.C. (Youth Minister In Charge). Let me explain.

Everyone loves a volunteer. You have jobs that demand lots of your time and still you find a way to give even more time to others. Any good pastor or church board member realizes that without you, there is no church. That's why you guys get banquets and pats on the back. You deserve every one of those things and more. What you don't often get, however, is the pointed finger. You don't always get to see the "underbelly" of the church. You don't often get to take the phone calls and the "I just happened to be in the neighborhood so I thought I'd stop by and chat with you" visits to your office. You're the volunteer, and the church usually feels lucky to have you.

Sometimes things change when a paycheck becomes attached to a ministry. I've been in both positions. I've been the volunteer who dreamed of earning a living doing this youth ministry thing. I've also experienced the reality of being a professional minister. They are two different worlds, trust me. As a paid staff member, you often see another side of the church. You sometimes see your pastor act more like a corporate boss than a spiritual leader. Occasionally, you hear the "sweet little old church lady" inform you that the last guy had more kids in his group. Monday through Friday, most churches are businesses with deadlines and meetings. (Lots of meetings.) What happened to water balloons, fart machines, and pizza all day, every day?

Having said that, let me tell you the one thing that makes this job the best thing you can do with your time. Every once in a while, you get to introduce someone to Jesus. Every once in a while, you get to experience the joy of a life changed and a soul saved. That makes it all worth it!

I still love Wednesday nights. Nothing jacks me up more than spending time with young people. When I lose that excitement, I'll get out. No one will have to tell me it's time to hit the road, I will already have headed towards the door. There is something indescribable about what happens in your soul after one of your teens hugs you, and tells you how much they appreciate you. (Getting called a dork and having stuff poured on you is the same as a hug in teen–world). Those moments will help you put up with the rest of the crap.

Those types of things have happened often in my career. I thank God for them because there have been times when I have been close to turning in my walking papers. I have had my share of pity parties when I felt under-appreciated. There was a time not too long ago when I began to question my sanity for sticking with this profession. Not even an hour later, I got a message on our youth group MySpace page that saved my career for the day.

"I just wanted to tell you how much I appreciate you. I know it seems like sometimes we aren't listening to you. But we are. My best friend has been coming to church now for a few weeks and she wants to keep coming. Thanks for putting up with us."

How often does Donald Trump hear that in his day?

2 You Are a Professional. Yes, You!

I will admit it. I am one of the sloppiest people on the entire planet. My desk, my car, and my house are usually in a state of anarchy that can only be described as "contemporary disaster zone". Most people, upon entering my office, will do a double–take at my desk. There are piles of paper, business cards, big gulp cups, and the stapler my office manger has been trying to locate for over a month. It's a state of organization that few are capable of understanding, except for the youth minister.

I know where everything is! If I conformed to the ultra-anal techniques of putting everything in file folders, I would spend more time looking for stuff. Believe me, I've read the books that try to convince you that you aren't really a professional unless you have everything filed alphabetically. I don't live alphabetically. I live with my head on fire. This works for me, and I've gotten to a place in my life and in my career where I feel comfortable saying that.

Keep a Neat Desk

After saying all that, let me give beginners a little advice: Keep a neat desk. You already have absolutely no respect! Don't give anyone fuel for cutting you down. Even if you usually have the urge to give people wedgies, do what you can to appear as professional as possible. If you are a hopeless slob like me, take these few pointers and try to hang on.

Dress Professionally

I've been fortunate enough to work for churches that have very loose dress codes. My first pastor never wore socks. Another of my pastors always wore Hawaiian shirts. My current one prefers to wear shorts and sandals. Even in these climates, I've chosen to come to work in slacks and polos. It's the easiest way to come across as a professional. Putting on a pair of slacks and buttoning a few buttons on a shirt is far easier than reading the *Wall Street Journal* every day. Do, however, take the opportunity to dress down *occasionally*. It will allow you to be part of the team.

Save the Fart Jokes for the Youth Group

In eight years, I've learned that most people really don't appreciate the humorous, subtle nuances of bodily functions. I've had the good fortune to work with some really fun pastors. (Pastors in general seem to be funny people.) But office staff, financial managers, and volunteers often don't possess the extra funny bone. Treat the people in your office like they are the grandparents of your new girlfriend. Always be polite and professional.

Don't Use Your Computer Like You're at Home

Not looking at porn should be a given. Once I was hired to replace a guy at a church who had just been busted for it. (Please don't think I'm saying that it's ok to look at porn at home either.) Use your computer for research. Use your computer to stay in touch with your young people. Use your computer to put together cool websites and newsletters. When you are on the phone being told how to do your job by a well-wishing church member, use it to play Minesweeper. DO NOT use it for personal e-mails or to find stuff for your car on eBay. Again, do us all a favor and leave the porn alone. "Church guys" who get caught for this stuff get their faces plastered all over the news. I'm sick of having to convince people that just because I work with young people at a church, I'm not a psycho.

Inform People of Your Whereabouts

Youth ministry isn't about being at your desk. Sometimes you are out visiting kids. Sometimes you are at Wal-Mart looking for whipped cream and cheap swim goggles. It's a great job if you like to be out and around. Most churches will expect you to have some office hours, however. Respect those hours. Understand this though: whenever you leave the office, it's your responsibility to be a good steward of your time. Letting someone in the office know where you are, and how long you expect to be, is a necessary form of accountability.

Honor Your Day Off

As a youth minister, you must have a day off during the week! Saturdays and Sundays are filled with activities and responsibilities. Don't let anyone tell you that you get weekends off just like everyone else: "Other people come to church on Sundays, why should you consider it work?" Because it is. They get to choose where they worship. You have to go to the church where you are employed (even if the music stinks). Consequently, so does your family. Any time you don't have a choice, its work! If you don't currently have a day off during the week, ask for one. You need time to be away from the church. You have to recharge, rest, and get ready for another week of ministry.

Make Appearances during the Day

If you have your own office, it's ultra-important that you come out of your cave every so often.

1. It helps break up the monotony of the day.
2. It reminds people in your office that you work there.
3. The coffee machine is usually located in another part of the building.
4. Saying the occasional "hello" to your pastor is a great way to maintain a good relationship.

Manage Your Time Wisely

One of the perks of this profession is that you probably don't have someone looking over your shoulder all the time keeping track of how you utilize your time. Because so much trust has been placed on your ability to do your job, it's important to make good use of the time you're being paid for. Here are some of the things I do to keep me accountable.

1. **Make a to-do list every day.** Start your day by thinking about the things you need to get done. Write them down and when you have completed them, jot down approximately how long it took you to accomplish the task. This visual will help you better prioritize the things you spend your time on. It's also a great tool to have at your disposal should someone ask "What is it that you do around here anyway?"

2. **Rank your tasks in order of priority.** Chances are that you might not have enough hours in the day to get everything done. Rank them by importance for the day, making sure that the vital tasks are at the top of your list. I always give priority to things like phone calls, visits, and study time ahead of things like looking through the mounds of junk mail and e-mail advertisements that I receive.

3. **Drop almost everything if your pastor requests something of you.** The pastor-youth minister relationship is vitally important. If your pastor asks for your opinion or to bring your tired carcass into his or her office, make sure it happens. Unless of course you are speaking to a parent or one of your students. Your pastor will understand and appreciate that they are your focus.

4. **Ask if there is anything else you should be doing.** Sometimes you don't know until you ask. Every once-in-awhile, make sure you ask your pastors, boards, congregation, students, and your parents if there is anything they wish you were doing that you presently aren't. It will go a long way in terms of proving to those important folks that you take your job seriously.

None of that was probably earth–shattering for you. But if you follow this advice, you may have a chance at hanging around. (Even if your desk looks like Office Depot threw up all over it.)

3 No Seminary Training? No Problem!

I didn't attend seminary to study youth ministry. In fact, my degree is in elementary education. After I graduated, I spent two years teaching fifth grade. I loved the kids, I loved teaching, and I was pretty good at creating lessons that didn't bore them to tears. But I found out something about myself: I didn't like teaching in the classroom. It was too confining. I couldn't bear the prospect of spending years in the same classroom, teaching the same curriculum. I needed to go onto something else.

During my second year of teaching, our school booked an organizational / motivational half–day seminar. The presenter was having the time of his life. He described the benefits of an organized notebook with the gusto normally reserved for your winning lotto numbers. This guy was amazing!

I approached him immediately after the presentation, and told him that I wanted to be part of his company. We continued the conversation over several months, and eventually I was hired as an educational / motivational speaker. It was a great gig! I was traveling all around the country, and I was making pretty good money. The seminars were short enough so that I could fly into the city at night, do the presentation the next morning, and be home in the evening. It was the perfect job for me.

Then came September 11th, 2001. Suddenly, traveling for a living lost its luster. I made the decision to quit after I was in the air headed to Washington D.C., of all places, only a couple of days after flights had resumed. I was faced again with having to find something else to do.

We had moved to a town near the Tampa International Airport so that I could zip in and zip out when I needed to. I got online one day and decided to take a shot at this youth ministry thing. I was lucky enough to spend years learning from a real ministry pro and I had led that group for six months as a volunteer when he left. It was worth a shot.

As providence would have it, a Methodist Church about three minutes from my house was looking for a youth minister. I typed up a resume and went right over to hand it to the pastor. He was kind enough to look at it and talk to me about the position. I'll never forget our brief conversation.

"We are at the point where we are ready to name a youth minister, but something tells me that I should pray about you." I thanked him for his consideration, and left knowing that I should still keep looking for a job. A few days later, he called me back with some surprising news. He wanted me to meet some of the youth and his youth worker team. If they liked me, he was prepared to offer me the position.

Our meeting went well and I began my ministry career at a downtown, historical church in Bradenton, FL. This was the beginning of what is turning out to be a wild, amazing, beautiful, tragic, topsy-turvy, exhausting, and exhilarating ride. A little while later, I wanted to hear directly from my pastor about which of my sparkling talents had led him to such a brilliant decision.

"I liked your resume, and the fact that you have had a number of great life experiences. But mostly you own your own house, and the other guy required a housing allowance." (Pride has no place in youth ministry!)

How does my story apply to you? I believe that God calls all types of people to youth ministry, for all types of reasons. Seminary and Bible School are wonderful places that produce amazingly qualified people for the ministry. However, they aren't the only places that can create great ministers. Never let anyone tell you that you can't do something that you have the heart and talent for. If you're the right person, the right church will be willing to train you. (It may require a lot of looking, a lot of convincing, or a lease with your name on it.)

Youth ministry is so much more than just teaching the Bible to students. It's a full-time job that often requires much more than just your midweek program. In short, youth ministry requires talents and gifts above and beyond what any professor can teach you. While seminary and Bible school may be the most logical place to start, it isn't necessarily a deal breaker.

4 Say Hello to Those People Who Live in Your House

Chances are that you will work for numerous pastors, have tons of students in your youth group, and see Reliant K more times in concert than you care to talk about. But you only get one family.

My first pastor was, and probably still is, a workaholic. He would get to the office at 5:30a.m. and not leave until the evening. I often wondered how he had the energy to do it. He also had a wife, a teenage daughter, and a son in the fourth grade. Somehow, he managed to coach his kids in sports and hang out occasionally with his wife.

Our two children were born while I worked for this church. I remember a conversation I had with my pastor just after the birth of Sarah, our oldest. "I will kick your butt if you don't spend enough time with that little girl," he said. "There is no time-clock here, enjoy your mornings with her. She won't be little all that long."

My first church was very cool for a lot of reasons, but this was my favorite part. I worked for a pastor who understood that a cookie-cutter schedule isn't necessary to get the job done.

If you have a family in this profession, you are going to be away from them. Twice a week, on average, I miss the precious bedtime routine with my kids. There are weekend trips, weeklong retreats, summer camps, and mission trips that take me away as well. I have missed trick-or-treat excursions, and even my own birthday, because of trips. It's a tough career on families.

My first pastor insisted that I take mornings with my kids, and this is something that I have continued to do throughout my career. If I interview at a new church, I make it very clear that early mornings belong to my children. I really appreciate it when I haven't had to rush breakfast and Sponge Bob with them. Now, before we go any further, let me get one thing straight. I am not, by any means, the world's perfect example of parenting. My goal is simple: I try to raise decent kids while staying sane. That's it.

Youth ministry is a draining job. Granted, it really isn't a physically demanding profession, but the mental part of the job is formidable. Teenagers have lots of conflict going on in their lives. School is demanding, relationships are challenging, and often their parents just aren't as present as they should be. Our job is to be a spiritual adviser, parent, friend, and therapist to our youth group. It's a 24-7 type of job. I have had phone calls at 1a.m. from a student who had just finished cutting herself. I know that you have probably had the same kind of stuff too. I know firsthand how difficult it is to be emotionally available to your youth group and congregation all day long, and then turn around and be emotionally available to your own family. There are times when I simply fail to be Super Dad. Honestly, there are times when I even fall short of Super Crappy Dad.

I do my best to take advantage of little moments. I love to grab my kids for unexpected hugs and tummy raspberries in the living room. I enjoy taking the kids to Dairy Queen in the middle of the week, just because.

And yes, at least a couple of times a month, my wife and I get a baby sitter and go out on dates. Still, I know that I am not always as present as I would like to be. Sometimes I just don't have the strength.

The key to any youth ministry family is your spouse. I am blessed to have a wife who not only works full time, but also helps with my youth ministry, organizes and leads worship for one of our services, and still finds the time to be an amazing mother. I struggle with being an average youth minister and a decent dad. My wife finds a way to be excellent at all of it. At least I was smart enough to marry well.

It is essential to work for churches that understand the importance of family. I once interviewed at a huge church that was on the cutting edge of ministry. You only heard from them if they contacted you first. Needless to say, I was pretty impressed with myself for being on the "A-list".

During the interview, I couldn't help but notice that the interviewer looked tired. He spent a lot of time going over the church's cutting–edge approach, and how many people attended their high energy, contemporary service every week. He took great pride in explaining that their youth ministry had grade level leaders. Each grade level had 20 to 30 students, Yada Yada Yada.

We got to a certain part of the interview (where he stopped talking long enough to take a breath) and I asked him simply, "How many hours per week does the average staff member put in around here?" He looked at me as though I had peed on his shoes. "I don't know, 60-90 hours I guess." He continued with the rest of the presentation and when he finished, I thanked him for meeting with me. I went home with a very easy decision to make.

My wife wanted me to take the job, and my mother-in-law definitely wanted me to take the job. It was in the same town as my wife's brother and family, and the money was really, really nice. When I came home, my wife was practically standing at the front door waiting for me to open it and share my reaction. It was easy to share.

"I'm not taking the job."

"What?"

"I don't want the job. I would never see you or the kids. 60-90 hours per week."

"Yeah, you shouldn't take that job."

I called the associate pastor back, thanked him for his time, and informed him that I wasn't interested. He paused, and informed me that no one had ever told him that they weren't interested in working at his church. I simply replied, "Working at your church sounds interesting, it's the dying at your church that I don't want any part of."

Involve Your Family If You Can

My two kids even get involved in my ministry. My 6-year-old daughter sometimes helps my wife and I set up games in the youth room for Wednesday night meetings. She is getting better at cleaning up, so we let her wipe down the dinner tables. My 4-year-old son is really good at running in circles and jumping up and down. I am still figuring out how to utilize these particular skills.

I am lucky. My wife teaches mathematics at the local high school and she is amazing with teenagers. She is the perfect compliment, because there are far more female students in my youth groups than male students. I don't care how talented you are as a male youth minister, there are things about adolescent females that you don't know, and will never fully understand. This is where my wife is invaluable. She is able to point out subtle changes in attitudes and personalities that I would usually miss. I can't count the number of times my wife has filled me in on situations with our female students that needed my attention. One of her God-given gifts is spotting budding romances. This brings us to the next chapter...

5   Love is in the Air, and It Isn't All that Beautiful

Teenagers fall in love more frequently than they change socks. We would all like to think that the only reason teens flock to our youth groups is because they have an unquenchable thirst for the Lord. Hopefully, they will get around to that.

I have a rule in my youth group that is completely unenforceable and ridiculously unrealistic. In fact, this rule has been ignored in my groups at an astounding rate of *all the freaking time!* The rule is, *no dating within the group.* (I told you that it was ridiculous).

At a youth ministry conference, I had a conversation with a guy who was studying to be a youth minister. He was set to graduate in a few months and he had a job lined up. We began to talk about our lives, and I told him the beautifully romantic story about my wife and I, and how we met each other at youth group. It was love (or lust) at first sight, for both of us. We dated from the moment we saw each other as high school juniors, and we have been together ever since.

This young man said that my story reinforced his opinion that the youth group is the perfect, safe place for young people to develop healthy attitudes about dating. Let me explain to you why I totally disagree with this line of thinking.

Christian Teens Have Raging Hormones Too

Those sweet little faces that look so angelic when they pray, are little balls of hormonal fury. Being a

Christian doesn't mean that you lose the ability to notice what a person looks like in a pair of jeans. We do our teens a great disservice when we take their urges for granted. I have had discussions with many parents about the sexual struggles of their kids. The phrase, "Not my kid, he/she is a Christian," has come up more times than I care to remember.

I'll share with you the real experience of a couple in one of my youth groups. For the sake of discussion, the female will be called "Bertha" and the male will be called "Pierre". I will use those names because they made me laugh, and also because I've never had a single Bertha or Pierre in any of my groups.

Bertha came over to our house one evening because she really needed to talk. She and Pierre had been dating for a couple of years, and they had recently given in to their sexual urges.

Bertha came from a strong Christian home. Both of her parents were involved in ministry, and her older sibling was the kid that everyone looked up to and admired. Bertha was convinced that she had ruined her life. How could she continue to claim that she was a Christian, she said, when she was doing something that she knew she shouldn't, and didn't know if she was strong enough not to do again?

Bertha became more withdrawn. She was still attending church and making the effort to appear happy, but it was easy to tell that she was in serious trouble. My wife and I continued to work with her closely. Eventually, I had a conversation with her parents about the situation. Yep, you guessed it, the "My kid is a Christian" argument took center stage.

Bertha was so riddled with guilt that she began to cut herself. The act of punishing herself gave her a momentary feeling of redemption. It was a vicious cycle. She didn't want to stop pleasing her boyfriend, but she also didn't like how she felt afterwards.

I am happy to report that God performed a miraculous work in her life. She went to a Christian counselor and, through prayer and determination; she was able to stop the cutting. She also summoned the courage to have a heart–to–heart talk with her boyfriend. She told him that she no longer wanted to base their relationship on sex. Unfortunately, Pierre didn't agree, and he broke up with her. She's now married and living very happily with a great man. By the grace of God, this story has a happy ending.

Teen Relationships Usually End Badly

As I mentioned before, my wife and I met as juniors in high school and we have been together ever since. I think that works out about 0.000000003% of the time. I share our story with my teens because it's a great story. I wish I had a dollar for every time a new dating couple has used it as a reason to date within the youth group. Sadly, break-ups happen and usually with damaging results.

Youth groups should be close-knit places where struggles and triumphs are shared. Teenagers are very good at developing close relationships. It's a beautiful thing when you can get a diverse group of people to come together to passionately serve God. It's also a traumatic thing to have that closeness torn apart by the need to "choose a side."

When two young people break up, it's usually done in cruel and immature ways. One of the relationships in my group ended when the guy decided that the best way to get his girlfriend to break up with his, was to simply stop talking to her. It worked; she did break up with him. But it started World War III in our group. Because they were two very popular kids, people chose sides. Consequently, not only did the former dating couple dislike each other, but now all the kids were at odds. We had life-long friends not speaking to each other over something that had nothing to do with them! Not a healthy situation.

Dating Teens Shut Themselves Off From Others

It happens all the time. Two people start dating and the flow of newly-ignored friends begins to stream into my office to tell me about it. "Murray was my best friend and now he won't hang out with me anymore! He's always with that girl!" It's a natural feeling to want to be around a person that you have developed romantic feelings for. They make your heart sing. The air smells fresh, the flowers look more vibrant, and High School Musical begins to really make sense!

Sometimes, it's not just friends who are ignored. Often, relationships become so all–consuming that school–work, family, clubs, sports, and other great things that used to matter are put on the back burner. The dating relationship can become an idol.

If you figure out how to enforce the "No Dating Rule", please let me know. Short of being able to enforce it, however, I have adapted something that has proven to be helpful. When I or my wife (usually my wife) notices that two people are heading down the road of love and fuzziness, I invite them to come in and talk to me. I don't forbid them to date, but I do attempt to put some realities in front of them.

1. I ask them to make every effort to keep their relationship with God first in their lives.

2. I ask them to actually schedule time for dates *within* their current schedule that includes family, friends, and school.

3. I ask them to treat each other with respect.

4. I ask them to consider whether they are mature enough to handle the break-up without causing war.

5. I beg them not to do it!

A Really Different Situation

College kids can be very useful parts of your ministry. Especially college kids who want to become youth ministers. It is part of your duty as a youth minister to pass on some of what you know to others, so when you get the opportunity to work with a younger person who has ministerial aspirations, do it!

The problem with college students is that high school kids tend to think they are extremely cool. Sometimes, so cool that they "fall in love" with them. It's important to set up guidelines for your ministry volunteers. Dating relationships between college freshman that are helping out, and high school seniors that are still in your group, can create real issues. I know some ministers that have asked their volunteers to step down while they were in the relationship. I'll leave that to your discretion. Understand, however, that it will occur if you utilize college help long enough.

6   Lock-in 101

I am writing this while recovering from one of my least favorite parts of youth ministry. In my book, this unspeakable act is one of the things that will take precious years from your life. This horrific part of ministry is the "all-nighter" or the "lock-in."

I have spoken to lots of youth ministers and their opinions vary from, "They are extremely effective" to, "I don't see the need for them." You can choose which side of the fence you fall on. Chances are, however, that you will do one of these things during your career whether you like it or not. I feel obligated to mention some things that have worked and some that haven't.

Plan More Activities than You Can Possibly Do

Nothing brings about an attack of the tired, crabby teen faster than boring them to tears. If you can keep their minds off of the fact that they aren't sleeping, you can get through these things.

Decide the Tone of the Event

You can conduct a lock-in that has spiritual significance. You can also plan lock-ins whose only purpose is to see how much pizza you can stuff into a body in a twelve hour period. My experience has led me to the conclusion that trying to sneak spiritual stuff into a fun-themed lock-in takes away from the important points you are trying to make. Games and silly lock-ins will have positives regardless. Most notably, they give your students the opportunity to introduce your ministry to friends that might not ever step foot inside a church. They also go a long way toward community building, if you can keep them from killing each other during the crabby moments.

Go as Extreme as You Can Afford

I like to have more junk food, candy, soda, etc. on hand than the average teen has ever seen. Nothing says, "This is special" more than creating a sugar-laced paradise. Providing you only do these things a couple times every year, you won't cause any lasting dietary damage. Another thing I have done is to rent a bounce house for the entire event. Sometimes, inflatable rental companies will give you a reduced rate, since you are offering to rent their equipment during slack times. Traveling lock-ins are another way to change things up. Have trusted families in your church agree to have food and activities ready at scheduled times during the event. (Good luck finding someone to take the 3a.m. to 5a.m. time slot.)

Create an Hour-by-Hour Schedule

Even if I don't stick to it exactly, an hourly schedule helps me keep things moving. Again, schedule more things than you can possibly do. It's reassuring to parents when they see you have put a lot of time and effort into the event, and know what their children will be doing at all times. However, you must be where you say you are going to be when you say you are going to be there. There is nothing worse than a family with an emergency trying to find you in the parking lot, after you have decided to head your group into Wal-Mart on the spur of the moment.

Permission Slips and Conversations with Parents you don't know

One of the purposes of a lock-in is to attract students who don't come to your youth group on a regular basis. When your students bring friends, make sure you get a phone number or an address beforehand. This way you can introduce yourself to parents, and inform them about rules and expectations. Permission slips should always be used so that you have contact information, in case you have to report a broken nose, or send a kid home for torching the boys' bathroom.

Over-Communicate the Event End Time

At the end of the lock-in, you and those who helped you will be unfathomably tired. There is nothing worse than having to wait on late parents when all you want to do is find your bed and remain temporarily comatose.

Separate Rooms for Sleeping

Should you decide to wimp out and plan time for sleep, make sure you have separate rooms for males and females. Also, ensure that you have two chaperones of the same sex for each room. And remember that you probably shouldn't fall asleep. Your responsibility is to make sure that everyone is safe at all times.

All right, you've set up lots of fun and crazy activities, you have more than enough junk food to make Ronald McDonald jealous, and you've made sure you have signed permission slips. Things should work out just fine, right? Keep in mind that the best laid plans of mice and men can go haywire.

During one of my first lock-ins, I experienced something that I didn't plan for. We were having a wonderful time! My students were participating in all of my planned activities, and everyone was safe and happy. During the night, however, I noticed that it was getting increasingly warmer. I thought that we were just being very active, and that when we all calmed down later on in the night, everything would be just fine.

At 3a.m., everyone just wanted to chill out and watch a movie. I looked at the thermometer and it read, "85 hot, stinking degrees!" (We had a really descriptive thermometer.) I had failed to ask about the air conditioning system. Our church had a system that used ice to provide cool air, and apparently, it shut off to remake ice during the early morning hours. We spent the rest of the lock-in outside on our church lawn. It was July in Florida, and it was cooler outside that it was inside.

I mention this to illustrate that the smallest of details can make a huge difference in your lock-in. Give yourself plenty of time to plan for the unplanned, and attempt to think of all possible problems before they arise. Trust me, you don't want a roomful of hot and sweaty teen-aged humans anywhere near you at 4 in the morning. They smell like a combination of wet dog and month-old hotdogs.

All right, you are still insane enough to want to do one of these things. What can you do to make these things fun? Here are some of my favorite ideas.

Clean (Non-Messy) Games

Knock it Off

Materials Needed: two 6 to 8ft folding tables, one paper or Styrofoam bowl for each student, about 100 wadded up tinfoil balls, a marker.

The Setup: each student will write their first name on the bowl around the outside wall of the bowl. (The bowl will be upside down for the game, so write the name accordingly) Tables should be set up facing each other lengthwise with about 6 to 8ft of space between the tables.) Each student will place their bowl at the front of their teams table. Once they place their bowls on the table, they aren't allowed to touch it again.

The Game: Each player then moves to the other side of their table facing the other team. An equal supply of foil balls are provided to each team. When the leader says "Go" each team throws their foil balls at the other team's bowls. When a bowl is knocked off, the person whose name is on the bowl is out of the game. The team who eliminates the other team first wins.

One Seat to the Right

Materials Needed: A chair for every person.

The Setup: The group sits in a circle of chairs.

The Game: This game was the "go-to" game of my good friend Jerry Gardner. The students in one of his groups would *beg* to play this game every week. The leader asks "If you've ever" types of questions. If the student can answer the question with a "yes", then they move one seat to the right. The goal is to get around the circle back to your seat, alone. Now the tricky part.

What happens when a student answers a question with a "no?" That student stays in their seat. You will then begin to have students that have to move one seat to the right to chairs that are already occupied. When that occurs, the student will sit on the lap of the person in the chair. You may get situations where you have several students sitting on each other in one chair.

For each question, the top person decides movement. Let's say that the top two people in the chair can answer with a "yes." That means they move to the next chair. The person who was on the top in the last chair would now be sat upon by the person they were just sitting on! Now, person #3 answers the question with a "no." He stays put and it doesn't matter what person #4's answer is. He/she can only move when #3 moves off of them. Like I said, the goal is to get completely around the circle back to your original chair, ALONE! If you get back to your chair in a stack, the game continues.

Wink Assassins

Materials Needed: 1 chair for every 2 people.

The Setup: Each person in your group will need a partner. Put 1 chair for every team of 2 into a circle. Now you have to find another single person. Namely you! You will also need a chair in the circle. Each team chooses one person to sit down on the chair. The other person in the team will stand behind them.

The Game: You are standing behind your empty chair. The people in the chair now have to look at you. Their partners behind them have to look down at the person in the chair with their arms at their sides. You will choose a person in one of the chairs to wink at.

Once you wink at them, it is their task to get out of their chair and into your chair without being tagged by their partner. If they succeed, then the person who is without a partner becomes the "winker". After a few rounds call "switch" so that the winkers can become escape artists. You can keep track of who gets out of their chair the most and who is most successful at keeping their partners in the chair. I've also given away prizes for the most creative method of getting out of the chair.

Do You Love Your Neighbor?

Materials Needed: A chair for every person *except* one.

The Setup: Place the chairs in a big circle with plenty of space. Pick someone in the group to be "IT" first.

The Game: The IT person approaches someone and asks, "Do you love your neighbor?" That person has a decision to make. They can say "Yes" or "No". If they say "yes", they and the person to their left and right have to get up and exchange chairs. While that is occurring, the person in the middle is also attempting to sit down. The person left without a chair is now the person asking the question. If the person answers "No", They have to tell about the types of people they DO love." For instance, "I DO love people who are wearing socks!" Now ALL of the people in the circle who are wearing socks have to get up and find an empty chair. Again, the person in the middle is also attempting to find a chair.

Psycho Simon Says

This is Simon Says gone crazy! In order to pull this one off you need to find a Simon that can give instructions REALLY quickly! You also need to have a few volunteers watching the crowd that is trying to do as Simon says. Simon starts off normally, then suddenly starts to bark off instructions at break-neck speed. A person is out if they START to make the wrong movement. Also, the crowd has to keep their eyes on Simon at all times. So Simon can be giving misleading gestures to throw them off. For example, if Simon says to touch your ears, he may elect to touch his nose instead. If the student attempts to touch their nose instead of their ears, they would be out. The key is to do what Simon SAYS...not what he DOES! Now do this at a really fast speed and throw in the occasional directions without Simon's approval, and you have some fun stuff.

Sweaty Games

Sardines

The Setup: This game is basically Hide and Go Seek in the *dark* with a twist. We like to play in teams of two. The first team picks a hiding spot while the rest of the teams are in another closed room.

The Game: after a predetermined amount of time, you let teams go out one by one until all the teams are out looking for the hiders. Here's the twist. When a team finds the hiders, they have to hide *with* them. Eventually you go from a large group of people hunting to just one.

The fun occurs when you actually find the team and have to hide with them. Most of our church is open to hide in when we play this, including the restrooms! It is hilarious to have 20 teenagers all hiding in one stall! The team that finds the hiders first gets to hide in the next round. The second team to find them gets to be let out first to go find the new hiders. You decide the order of the hunters by what place they came in finding the hiders in the previous round.

Capture the Flag

Materials Needed: 2 dish towels.

The Setup: Divide your group into two equal teams. Take them outdoors to actually play the game. Each team has their "side" of the field. They are completely safe on their side of the field. In the middle of the field create a neutral zone. Everyone is safe in the neutral zone. Before the game begins, each side must decide where it will hide their dish towel (flag). It has to be in within reach of even the shortest members in the group. Each side also sets up an area on their side of the field that will designated as their "jail".

The Game: When the game begins each team must figure out a strategy to find the other team's flag. To capture the flag, members from each team must venture into the other team's side of the field. The object of the game is to find the flag without being tagged by the other team on their side of the field. If you get tagged in the attempt to find the flag, you are carted off to jail. Each team is allowed one person to guard the jail. The more people you can put in jail, the easier it is to find the flag for your team. There is always a "twist", however. If a person in jail gets tagged by one of their teammates, they then become free and can rejoin the hunt for the flag. If a person makes it successfully into the neutral zone, they cannot be tagged. The neutral zone gives you an opportunity to rest a little and try to visually locate the flag. The team that finds the other team's flag, captures it, and brings it back to the neutral zone is the winner.

Stomp

Materials Needed: A few blown up balloons for each student and string.

The Setup: Each student starts with one balloon tied with string around an ankle. The string should be long enough so that the balloon hangs safely enough away from the ankle to avoid stomping. Divide your students into two equal teams. In order to help keep the teams straight, use only two different colored balloons. When the leader says "Go" each person will attempt to stomp on the balloons of the other team.

The Game: The goal is to burst your opponent's balloons before they burst yours. The team that busts the all of the others first is the winner. **IMPORTANT!!!** Make sure that shoes are off for this game.

Just Plain Weird Games

Bobbing for Poo Poo

Materials Needed: 1 kiddy pool filled halfway with water, yellow food coloring, a couple of bags of chocolate-nutty bite sized candy bars.

The Setup: You are definitely going to want to do this one outside. Take your kiddy pool filled halfway with water and add your yellow food coloring until you get the desired color you're looking for. Unwrap your candy bars and float them in the pool. You can play this game with about 10 students per round. Line your students up around the pool with enough room so that they don't bump skulls. Each student is blindfolded with their hands behind their backs.

The Game: When the leader says "Go" each student will begin bobbing for (i.e. trying to capture with their mouth) the chocolate bars. Set a time limit and the student who has caught the most chocolate bars is declared the winner. I usually give out a family sized package of toilet tissue for the winners, although you may want to make sure this doesn't get used for mischief.

Gross Food Relay

Materials Needed: 2 brown paper grocery bags, assorted "gross" foods, 2 adult volunteers.

The Setup: This is another "outside is best" kind of game. Divide your students into two equal teams. You will want to make sure you have at least one food item per team member in the bag. Also, make sure that you have the same items in each bag.

The Game: The students will line up in a single file line and take turns choosing something out of the bag without looking. It is a good idea to wrap each item up so that it is harder to determine what it is by touch. (If you are playing this game during Christmas time, you can gift-wrap each item) Each team will have an adult volunteer that will serve as bag holder and official judge. One by one, the student will approach the bag and choose an item. That student has the choice of eating that item or putting it back into the bag to choose another one.

However, The student *must* eat the next item they choose. When the judge has declared that an item is eaten completely the student will return to the line and the next student will approach the bag. The team that finishes the contents of their bag first wins. It is a grand idea to have a large trash can available for each team. Just in case, um…the food makes a rather unappetizing return. (Make sure you are knowledgeable about food allergies in your group should they exist. Also, try not to make the foods so gross that your students won't participate.)

Cheeto Head

Materials Needed: Shaving cream, swim goggles, a chair for each team and crunchy corn cheese snacks (Cheetos)

The Setup: Divide your group into two equal teams. Each team will appoint a person to sit in the chair. When that person is seated, have them put on the swim goggles. After the goggles are correctly put on, apply a healthy amount of shaving cream to their head. (Enough to cover their hair) Give every other member a handful of Cheetos. The team should circle around the seated person and remain about two feet away from them at all times

The Game: When the leader says "Go" the team will start tossing Cheetos at the shaving cream covered head. Set a time limit and at the end of the allotted time, the team with the most Cheetos stuck to the shaving cream covered head wins.

These are just a few of my tried-and-true lock-in games. There are a number of great games books and websites that can help you find even more crazy games!

Downtime Activities

You can't keep your students running at breakneck speed for the entire night. It is wise to have a few more restful things planned at various times during the night. One of the best things to do is to show an appropriate movie. Make sure that the movie is age-appropriate for your group. Also, never just trust the ratings system. Always pre-screen the movie yourself before you show it. The trick is to find a movie that your kids will enjoy and that your parents won't be knocking on your door about the next day.

Themed Lock-Ins with a Purpose

Sometimes, it's A-OK to have a lock-in that is nothing but fun. They are great group building events and they also are effective "foot-in-the-door" events for your students to invite those friends that might have not ever been to church before. Your lock-ins can also have a spiritual tone to them as well. Once a year we have what we call a "missions lock-in." We play a few games, but the majority of the time is spent doing good deeds for others. During our last missions lock-in, we picked up trash on the road that our church is located on and we helped our local food pantry sort out their donated items. The most important thing we did, however, will stick with them forever.

There is an amazing young couple in our church that suffered the loss of their first child just days after his birth. Our church planted a tree with a name plaque on our grounds in his honor. I spent about 15 minutes introducing this family and their story to our kids via a PowerPoint presentation. At the conclusion of the presentation, I invited them to write messages from their hearts to the family. We attached the notes with colored ribbon to the tree so that when the family arrived to church the next morning, they could be encouraged by the kindness of our students. I asked my group if they would grant me permission to read the notes, which they did. The depth and the love that was relayed in those messages was something that made me extremely proud of them. It was a small act that affected not only the family of this child, but every member of our youth group.

Hopefully, your lock-in will be an event that your kids will be talking about for a long time. Just make sure you remove all evidence of the food fight that broke out in the sanctuary.

The Best Lock-In Movies

10 Movies with a Teachable Message

10. *Star Wars* (good vs. evil, "the force", lots of good teachable moments)
9. *A Christmas Story* (family, the simple things in life)
8. *Rudy* (hard work, persistence)
7. *It's a Wonderful Life* (everyone is important)
6. *The Wizard of Oz* (Friendship, being happy with what you have)
5. *Field of Dreams* (family, following your dreams)
4. *Rocky* (hard work, love conquering all)
3. *Mr. Holland's Opus* (finding your place)
2. *Pride of the Yankees* (courage, strength, grace)
1. *The Rookie* (courage, persistence, family)

10 Movies Just for Fun

10. *Spaceballs*
9. *Finding Nemo*
8. *Harry Potter*
7. *Monsters, Inc.*
6. *The Princess Bride*
5. Old school monster movies (*King Kong, Dracula, Frankenstein, Godzilla,* etc.)
4. *The Incredibles*
3. Blooper reels (sports, movie outtakes)
2. *Kung Fu Panda*
1. *The Lion King*

Sample Lock-In Plan

7pm	Check in and collect permission slips and money (If you've charged for it)
7:30pm	Feed the students
8:00pm	Outside game time
9:00pm	
10:00pm	Inside game time
11:00pm	
12:00am	Just plain weird game time
1:00am	Movie time
2:00am	
3:00am	Board games or other more restful activities
4:00am	Snack time and caffeine intake
4:30am	Outside game
5:30am	Inside game
6:00am	Breakfast time
6:30am	Cleanup
7:00am	Time to go home!

7 Success to Some May Look Like Failure to Others

What does a successful youth ministry look like? To most youth ministers, success means helping our students grow and mature in their relationships with Christ. I think that everyone who has any interest at all in youth ministry would agree. Often however, other, less important, factors are looked at as determiners of success. Success in ministry is truly in the eye of the beholder.

Churches rely on contributions in order to survive. Without the tithes and offerings, none of us would have buildings to work in, programs to create, or pizza to eat on Wednesday nights. Traditionally, Sunday morning attendance by teenagers determines whether a youth program is doing its job. For many of us that may seem unfair, but it makes sense. Most members of any given congregation aren't around when youth group occurs. If a church sees teenagers coming to worship on Sunday, it must mean that the youth minister is doing his or her job.

Good theory, but it's dead wrong. The church of today is vastly different than it was just a decade ago. The church isn't the focal point of community life. The church is hardly the focal point in many families who would be highly upset if you classified them as anything other than Christian. Church attendance has become merely part of the week. It may be a very important part of the week, but it's still only a part.

The truth is that youth attendance at Sunday morning worship has more to do with the Sunday morning programming than it does with the overall health of the youth ministry. Gone are the days where most families attend one church for everyone's spiritual needs. It has become very common for a teen to attend a youth group at a different church than the one at which their family worships on Sunday. It's not even unusual to find faithful youth group members who belong to a family that doesn't attend church at all. In the past, it may have been true that a successful youth ministry's main responsibility was to teach confirmation, and organize the yearly mission trip. But the stakes have been raised dramatically.

I am blessed to work for a very forward thinking church. I work with two pastors who work their backsides off to promote new ways of thinking towards Christianity and the way it is presented. We aren't all about numbers. We *are* all about making a difference in the lives of young people. I pray that you get to work for a church that approaches your ministry the same way. Fortunately, the tide is changing. More and more churches are beginning to understand that focusing on the ministry will result in the numbers they want to see. The conversation is about how the world is changing, and how the approach of the church — not necessarily the message —needs to change along with it.

A common misconception is that youth are looking for crazy games, comfortable teaching, and "extreme" attempts to occupy their time. Time in Teen-world is at a premium. The church should be a place of refuge and peace, not a place that adds to the "busyness" of life. Some groups are still working under the premise that "more is better." I've taken a look at many youth group websites around the country, and it seems as though their goal is to fill every available free second of their teens' lives. I'm not sure that accomplishes anything other than burnout.

Here is a crazy thought. The next time someone asks you what you have planned to enhance the life of the youth in your ministry, offer them this.

"We are shortening the length of midweek youth group. We believe that our students need a place to hang out, unwind, and be themselves, so we are going to commit a space in the church that belongs to youth, and youth alone. We are going to teach the Scripture in a way that challenges and alarms our youth. We are also eliminating Sunday night youth meetings, because we feel that our youth need more family time. We are committed to planning no more than one activity per Saturday, and absolutely none of them are going to be wasted in trying to raise a buck."

8   Treating "Senioritus"

There is an incurable condition out there that is affecting your high school senior. While it isn't fatal, it does have very real affects on the student, their parents, and your mental health. This condition is known as "Senioritus". Senioritus affects nearly 100% of those entering their final year of high school. There is no known cure, only ways of treating the symptoms.

What Are the Symptoms?

Senioritus has some tell-tale symptoms, they include;

1. The sudden onset of the dreaded "Know-It-All's"
2. The sudden onset of the dreaded "I Can't Wait to Get Out of Here's"
3. The sudden onset of the dreaded "I'm too Busy/Tired to Participate's"
4. The sudden onset of the dreaded "I'm Too Mature to Hang Out With These Children's"

Senioritus can drastically affect the dynamic of your ministry. But, be aware that the effect it is having on the student's parents is even more drastic.

Parent's Suffer Greatly through Senioritus

Children are parent's greatest gifts. They are both their greatest source of joy and their greatest source of pain. They are the ultimate "Riddle wrapped within an enigma." Up until the senior year, students typically rely heavily on their parents. Sure, they have the arguments and moments of craziness, but typically mom and dad are sources of needed stability. Something happens when a person enters their senior year.

The battle for independence escalates significantly. Being on their own was a far off dream for their entire lives. But now, they can see independence around the corner. As each day passes in the student's senior year, that independence becomes clearer. Seniors are preparing for a time when mom and dad won't be around all the time to tell them what to do. This isn't an easy reality for parents to face.

Parents love to be needed by their children. They battle with the reality of knowing that their children will someday need to stand on their own two feet, and with the memories of how beautiful it was to have their children rely on them. Parents can take solace in this fact; your children will *always* need you! In fact, during their senior year, they need you more than ever.

How Parents Can "Be There" For Their Seniors

This is difficult because the level that senior students want their parents to be there for them changes almost instantly. High school seniors desire to be treated like adults. That means giving your senior options instead of simply telling them what to do. Now, when you give them options, will they always do the right thing? Of course not! We adults still struggle with doing the right thing, don't we? This is where being the parent continues to bring joy. When they make good decisions, be right there to congratulate them. When they make poor decisions, be right there to help them dust off. This isn't the time for "I told you so!" Instead, poor decisions are great times of teaching. Sit down with them and talk about how choosing a different approach may have led to a different outcome.

Sadly, I've seen parents become even more overbearing in response to their seniors. Instead of giving options, I've seen parents try to tighten the grip on their children. The old attitude of "While you're under my roof, you'll live under my rules" is often the response I've witnessed. While I agree that seniors still need to follow the rules of the house, there has to be some recognition that your little baby is actually a young adult. You've done a great job of preparing your student to be an independent adult. Now it's time to let them practice that while you are still around to help them out.

There is a fine line between letting them practice being an adult and completely washing your hands of parenting. It is difficult to find the happy medium. When I was a senior, my parents basically removed all of the rules. They no longer asked me when I would be home or what I was up to. Believe me, I took full advantage of that situation. I was old enough to know right from wrong, but I wasn't mature enough to fully understand the consequences of my actions. I did some things that were dangerous and down-right stupid. By the grace of God, I lived through them.

Many seniors aren't that lucky, however. It seems like there is an "In Memory of" page in every high school year book. While I was a junior in high school, we lost one of our seniors to a drunk driving accident. This student was coming home after a party in a Baja type of jeep with no roof. The driver of the jeep had been drinking and was driving at a high speed. The

driver hit something in the road and the impact pro-
jected the girl out of the vehicle. She wasn't wearing a
seat belt and she died instantly. Tragedies like this are
all too common among our high school seniors. As
parents, you must find the doable balance between
giving your child independence and imposing the rules
of the house.

The Senior-Youth Minister Relationship

We've talked about the senior-parent relationship,
but what about those seniors and the youth minister?
There are some special things that we youth leader type
get to experience as well.

Seniors Can Be Great to Have Around

While it's true that they typically pose some special
challenges, they also exhibit some pretty cool stuff too.
High school seniors tend to become pretty enjoyable to
hang around. They have a more mature sense of humor. There are times when you can sit down with your
seniors and talk to them like adults. They are beginning
to understand that life is more than just dances and
cool clothes. It's very rewarding to see them begin to
put the stuff you've been teaching them into practice.
One of the greatest joys you will have is when they get
in touch with you from college to tell you how something you said to them years ago finally makes sense!

Seniors Can Be a Great Source of Leadership

While it's true that some seniors remain very involved in your ministry until they graduate, a lot of
them will show diminished participation. That doesn't
have to be a total negative. Instead of writing seniors off

as being "past your group", look at the time they give you as a positive.

Dale Murphy was my favorite baseball player while I was growing up. He had an amazing mix of power and speed as an outfielder. Dale was a deeply spiritual man and also a very quiet type of leader. He tended to let his play on the field speak for him. I've read of the times when he did choose to speak up in the locker room. Because it didn't happen very often, it tended to have a very powerful affect on his team. Your seniors can have the same type of affect on your youth group. While it's true that they may not be there as often as you'd like to exhibit their leadership, the times they are there to exhibit their leadership will be powerful and meaningful times for your entire group. Like their parents, you have instilled great things in them. It's a pleasure to see them come out.

Your seniors may not show it, but they are struggling with letting go. Yes, they may want to talk about nothing but how cool their new dorm mate is, or how much they can't wait to be away from home, but they are still going through a ton of anxiety. As their youth minister, you have an inside track on how to help them.

1. Remind Them From Time to Time that You're Going to Miss Them.
2. Use moments to share some personal stories about your senior year transition.
3. Remind them to spend some time with their parents.
4. If they have younger siblings, remind them that they are going to miss them too. Encourage them to spend time with each other.

5. Be understanding when they aren't there. Don't chastise them for missing youth group. Instead, give them a big hug when they do show up.

6. Remind them that you are going to be praying for them every day.

Think about that really corny line from the Whitney Houston song *The Greatest Love of All* (1985) and change it to read "I believe the seniors are our future." If you do that, you will have done your part in helping to save the world. This planet needs more well-taught people with beautiful insides.

9 Important Things to Remember About Ethics

Maybe some of you are parents to little ones. I am, and I have learned that the skill of rule making is an invaluable one to possess. In logical, sane-thinking, adult world it seems to be a matter of the obvious to know the basic rights from wrongs. I'm quite sure that you have never been handed an employee handbook with the "There shall be no spitting of milk at anyone above the shoulders" clause. Being a parent, however, such rules are all too necessary.

Much of the same applies to youth ministry. When I first entered ministry I tried to use the very huggy and fuzzy theories that I had learned as an education major. I was taught that too many classroom rules were just plain ole' negative. Instead, we were taught to institute policies such as "Always show the proper respect for each other." Another favorite of mine was, "Share, Care, and Nair." (I don't think it was actually Nair, I can't remember the last silly rhyming word.) I think you get the picture.

At first glance, these simple rules follow the lines of the Golden Rule. "Do unto others as you would have done unto you." Simple, sound, and Biblical. That really should be all you need in terms of setting up boundaries in your ministry, right?

Come on! The golden rule is advanced spiritual mindset. We have lessened its scope with the sing-song way we use to teach it to children. (How many of you are actually bobbing your head and singing "Do unto others as you would have done unto you?") Treating others with respect and policing your own behavior is heady stuff. 99% of adults don't ever master it. Your youth ministry needs specific guidelines, a code of ethics if you will.

Ethical Standards for the Youth Minister

We'll start with you. There are things you, as the head dude or chick in charge need to agree to.

Relationships with youth, parents, and volunteers are to remain professional. Understand that "professional" in the youth ministry world is a little different than "professional" in the corporate world. There are some things that apply to both, however. Romantic relationships with students are an obvious no-no. Even if he or she is 18 and considered by law to be an adult. It is a conflict of interest to do so. It also is just icky.

Romantic relationships with parents, providing both of you are single, is a little hazier subject. Personally, I wouldn't recommend it. It takes the relationship of you and that student from "youth minister-student" to "guy/girl my mom/dad is dating-student". The relationships are completely different. Dating volunteers is even hazier. My wife happens to be one of my volunteers. She isn't, however on any of my youth decision making boards. It would be an unfair proposition to put her in the situation where she might have to criticize me professionally. Also, what happens when romantically involved people have disagreements? Often they have unkind words, gestures, or body language towards each other. The last thing your students need is to have a tiff spoil their youth group experience. If you are in a mature relationship where both people involved are capable of solving their differences in privacy, then I can't really make much of an argument against it. However, this requires that you are capable of being totally unbiased on this judgment.

Flirting With Students Shouldn't Happen. You're young, maybe not that much older than your juniors and seniors. You try not to show favoritism but that certain guy or girl in your group is just so darn cute! You don't mean anything by it, and you certainly aren't going to take it to a physical level. It doesn't hurt anyone, right? I think it does. When you give a student more attention than you give the others it sends a negative message to the rest of the group. The rest of your students' worlds are governed by popularity. Your youth group should be a place where everyone is getting the proper respect and love. Honestly, there will be students in your groups that you will get along with or have more in common with than others. That's human and also why you need helpers with different types of personalities and interests as you. The more eclectic your troop of volunteers are, the more likely every student in your group will have an adult they can feel comfortable confiding in.

Always Have a Witness with You When you Counsel Teens or Parents. We live in a world of litigation. What you intended to be totally innocent can be misconstrued into something else by another person. There have been many youth ministers that have lost their jobs and their credibility over an accusation. Sadly, an accusation doesn't even have to be true in order to wreck your career! Consequently, it is absolutely essential that you always have someone else present, preferably the same sex as the student or parent you are counseling, in the same room or immediate space. It's absolutely necessary protection. Aside from protection, it's also quite valuable to have another opinion handy. If you miss the mark with advice it's always nice to have someone else there that might be able to help.

Maintain Your Spiritual Health. Make sure that you are being fed spiritually. Take the opportunities to get away to youth minister training and retreat type events. Ask for a Sunday every so often to be able to go and worship at another church. Find one that you can be anonymous in. A church that you can feel free worshipping and cleansing your soul in where you don't have to worry about what the little old lady across the aisle thinks. If you are spiritually empty, how can you expect to feed your students?

Ethical Standards for Your Group

Every youth group should have an understanding of what's considered over the line. Your rules are going to be different according to the needs of your students, your ability to lead, the wishes of your congregation and parents, and what your pastor tells you to do. There are some standards that are pretty universal.

Bullying or Put-Downs Will Not Be Tolerated. Your students come to your group to be safe. They should feel totally comfortable with exposing their souls in your ministry. If you allow students to laugh at or cut down other students during the serious times, you are permitting some very serious damage to occur.

A situation occurred in my youth group not too long ago that unfortunately had some negative conse-quences. A family in my group went through a very ugly and messy divorce. The divorce tore the heart out of my student. This student was a very popular person in our group with many friends. The divorce changed the student's personality. This student went from being kind and tender-hearted to angry and hard to be around. One night, this student lashed out at some friends with some very harsh language. Unfortunately, the friends of my student didn't understand the hell that was being experienced. Instead of understanding the situation, the friends took the insults to heart and stopped speaking to my student. The personality change was short-lived, but the friendships didn't rebound as quickly as they needed to. This student went from being a core member of my group to a student who rarely attends. We are currently working hard to help mend the fences, but hurt feelings can be slow mending things.

No One is allowed to Show Up "Messed Up" Drugs and alcohol and those under the influence of it shouldn't be put up with. I'm not saying that those kids aren't worthy to be ministered to, because they are. Youth group time is not the place for it though. A messed up kid can pose serious safety risks for your group. I don't even want to think about the possibilities of having a kid who was messed up giving another kid a ride home or something similar to that. Be diligent. If you suspect that drugs or alcohol might be involved, call mom or dad immediately.

Suspicion of Abuse. A few years ago, I had a situation in my group where one of my parents called my house at night to tell me that their son/daughter was "out of control" and didn't want to talk to anyone but me. I went over there and observed that his/her eye was red and starting to turn blue and that there were obvious red marks on his/her wrists. I asked what happened and the reply was, "My dad grabbed me and hit me." Under the laws of the state I was in, I was obligated to report it to the child protection agency.

Obviously, this damaged the relationship between those parents and me. It also changed the way the student viewed me too. I lost a little bit of trust with him/her. Understand that the laws that protect the privacy between pastor and person don't apply to you if you aren't ordained. I have also witnessed situations where students where damaging themselves in various ways. I am always obligated to report this to parents, no matter how much the student objects. As a parent, I would want the same.

Create your standards, express them, and enforce them. Your ministry and stress levels will be much more to your liking.

10 Sometimes, Good Kids Make Bad Choices

Tonight was a particularly difficult night in my youth ministry career. I was informed during the day that a seventh grade girl in my city died accidentally while playing "The Choking Game." A couple of kids in my group were good friends with her. Even those that did not know her were overcome with emotion and doubt because stuff like this is not supposed to happen to one of their own. We learned a lesson tonight; sometimes, good kids make bad choices.

I wish I had a magical response to these types of situations, one that will make everyone reap the full benefits of all the possible lessons that should be learned. I just do not possess that magic. In fact, at time I do not even possess an answer that gives me a whole lot of comfort. I know it is even harder for my youth to find comfort in the answer.

What is the response? What can we tell our kids when they go through something horrific? Here it is; *God is present.*

I have to admit, that this answer does not always do it for me. Maybe I am not "churched' enough. Maybe my faith is not strong enough. When a beautiful, vibrant, and loved twelve year old girl makes one bad choice that she will never be able to fix; it just does not seem right. How can innocent twelve year old girls die from one unfortunate decision while many evil and perverse adults continue to hurt people and live to hurt more?

God is present.

That's it God? Is that all you have for us? Can your presence really be the best you can do? This thought takes me to an angry place until I remember this.

God is hurting too.

I know my Lord feels this pain. He bore the sin of the world on his shoulders at Calvary. He asked his Heavenly Father to forgive those who beat and mocked him. He wept when he spent time with families who were grieving. He experienced the pain that came along with denial and betrayal. He stood up for the sinful adulteress. My Lord knows what this feels like because He has always been present.

The Christian recording artist, Natalie Grant, sings a song that has helped me put these feelings into perspective. The song is titled, "Held"

We often feel as Christians that we are entitled to salvation from the bad things in life. God never made that promise. Never once did He tell us that life as a Christian would somehow be free from pain and suffering. Actually, He told us the opposite. He told us that we should expect persecution and trials. Sin has a very real place in our world and often it hurts those that we wish it would not.

Sometimes there just are not words that make the pain go away. Sometimes all we can do is cry in the arms of our Lord, Jesus.

God is present. Thank you, God.

11   It is Time to Celebrate Success!

Let's play a little word association. Just say the first word that pops into your head after you read the bold words below.

- **Severe Head Trauma**
- **Bamboo Thorns under the Fingernails**
- **Foot Crushed by Falling Planet**
- **Yearly Job Evaluation**

I bet all of those words had basically the same response in common. "Ouch", "Akkk" or "Oooh Man" would probably be among the most common. How sad is it that the tools we use to evaluate each other cause such painful results? Why do evaluations tend to stink? Evaluations tend to focus more on the negative than the positive. Our way of thinking dictates that we "have to fix the problems right away!"

When do we get to celebrate success in our life? How often do you hear about the strengths of your ministry? I sincerely hope you work for a church and pastors that make it a point to tell you how valuable you are. What if programs focused more on the positive? Does this seem improbable? Read on.

The Process of Appreciative Inquiry

David L. Cooperrider and Suresh Srivastava developed Appreciative Inquiry (AI) into a recognizable organizational tool in the 1980s. AI states that organization should be "a miracle to embrace rather than a problem to solve." In other words, your ministry plan should focus on the miracles and joys rather than the things that need to be fixed. A basic definition for AI is "that which gives life to basic human systems when they are functioning at their best."

AI centers around four basic processes.

1. Discovery
2. Dream
3. Design
4. Destiny

Discovery

You are attempting to bring out some of the best success stories from your ministry with a series of guided questions. These questions should be asked to a group of people who have different interests in your ministry. For example, my AI group includes parents, students, people in our congregation without kids, and even some church staff. Each of them brings their own ideas of what is important to the table. The questions are designed to be answered in the form of a great memory rather than a cold, matter-of-fact response. Questions like these may spark some interesting discussion among your youth council

- What was the highlight of our ministry year?
- Describe a moment that was incredibly meaningful to you
- Whom do you want to thank?
- What is our greatest strength?
- What makes our congregation happy about us?
- What is the most important factor that gives life to this ministry?

You may be somewhat of a skeptic, like me, and think, "How does this tree hugging stuff solve anything?" Believe me, it works. When you start telling people how much they matter, they will be much more willing to work on the areas that need improvement. Imagine at your next evaluation if you heard the phrases "What things need our attention?" or "What is God calling us to do?" instead of "Shape up or ship out!" or "You just are not meeting our expectations."

Dream

There is a difference between dreaming and "living in fantasy land." Dreaming involves scenarios that could happen if only the available parts would fit together in the right ways. Fantasy land involves parts and scenarios that do not exist and would never fit together.

Example- "I wish our youth group had 100 more members in it." This is a dream because it involves a scenario that could happen should the proper circumstances occur.

Example- "I wish I was making a million dollars a year as a youth minister." Now you are not only living in fantasy land, but you've fallen off of Mt. Fantasy and you've landed on your head, several times.

Let's think about what could happen this year if we worked together as a team and let God really change our lives and the lives of the youth among us. That is the beginning of the DREAM stage of the process.

Design

This is where your team makes the decisions about what really should be in your group. You've talked about the great things you've accomplished and about the awesome stuff you want to achieve. Now it is time to recreate the way you do stuff so that it falls right in line with the two. This is when you decide how things should be.

Destiny

Here is when all of that inspiration turns into action. This is typically the stage in the process when you start creating events, rules, programs, etc. AI is an ongoing process. That means you simply start over with an entirely new set of successes to share, dreams to reach for, and decisions to agree upon.

The Proof is in the Pudding

AI works because people love to be inspired. Think about any really good sports movie. What makes it so great? It undoubtedly has a main character who has to overcome monumental odds. They get there through hard work, a commitment to dream the impossible, and the wherewithal to make it all happen. Hardly ever does the main character reach the unthinkable goal by being constantly belittled. Those things may happen, but they aren't part of the success. They are typically part of the odds to overcome.

Why would we ever want to add hurdles for our ministries to jump over? Doesn't life supply enough of those already?

Reward People with What Energizes Them

Chances are, you have experienced the following situation

"Alright, alright, everyone needs to listen. Last year we didn't raise enough money to meet our budget. That means this year, Johnson, you are going to have to work twice as hard to get us across the line!"

(Johnson is looking at his shoes, shaking his head)

"Johnson! Are you even paying attention? Are you aware that your job relies on the money we bring in? If you care about your job, you better start giving a little more effort in the fundraising department!"

What the screaming guy fails to realize is that Johnson probably can't devote any more time or effort to fundraising. Johnson is contributing his maximum available effort and passion for fundraising. The problem is, he hates it. Therefore, he isn't all that good at it. Poor Johnson.

The goal is to get the job done right? Who cares if Johnson does it or if Smith gets it done? Maybe Smith likes fundraising. Stands to reason that Smith would do a better job if he has passion for it.

Maybe Smith is doing something that Johnson really loves to do. The problem is Smith is the Children Minister and Johnson is the Youth Director. They can't do parts of each other's job, can they?

Why not? They are on the same team, right? Assign people tasks that energize them. You will be amazed at how far the ball gets carried when it's handed to the right person!

PART II

Working with the Church Community

"Love the Lord your God with all your heart and with all your soul and with all your mind and with all your strength."

Mark 12:30 (*NIV*)

12 I'll Take "The Interview Process- The Professional Equivalent to the Root Canal" for 500, Alex

Before you get to settle all comfy like into your office chair, baptize your new youth room with soda and string cheese, and create your first monthly newsletter, you will need to get hired. In a perfect world, pastors would immediately realize how lucky they are to have the opportunity to be in your presence. On this planet, however, you will have to go through the interview process. This little bundle of wonderfulness can cause many sleepless nights and worry as you ask yourself, "Why haven't they called me back?" The process is usually long and tedious and performed by amazing people who are probably doing this in their spare time. Consequently, the hiring process in a church can seem like it lasts longer than the time Jesus spent with His Disciples. How can you help the church realize that you are the one they are looking for?

Get Your Name Out There

Most churches, like other businesses, use the internet to gather resumes. It is vital that you put together a strong online resume. It says a couple of things about you. 1. You are computer literate. 2. You are resourceful. 3. You are capable of being (or acting) professional. One very useful website is www.resumebear.com. Resume Bear is a free online resource that enables the user to create a professional looking resume, include a headshot to personalize the resume, and they provide a tracking tool that tells you exactly when a prospective employer opens your resume and how much time they spend looking at it. It even has an option where you can write a cover letter and include a link in the letter to your resume so they can open it right away.

Make sure that your resume is in the spots where churches are looking. For youth workers this is Youth Specialties. You can upload your resume free of charge to their "Jobs" section. Most youth professionals find their jobs through this site. Another site with a free jobs section is www.youthpastor.com. You should also check to see if your denomination has a website that covers the churches in your district. Often, these sites will include job openings for their local churches. Finally, don't forget about Craigslist! Many churches are now taking advantage of this free resource as well.

Memorize the Names You Hear

You will hear about a zillion names during the interview process. Each time you talk to someone, make sure you know exactly whom you spoke to and what responsibility he or she carries out in the church. When you are called back for those second, third, and fourth interviews, being able to put a name to a face may separate you from the rest of the crowd. Also, always remember to thank people for the time they spend with you. Remember, these people are more than likely volunteering their time to the church.

Dress for Success

This is not the time for that cool "Stay Puft Marshmallow Man" t-shirt you just found on eBay. Save that for youth night.

Men: Properly fitting button up shirt with collar. Tuck it into a khaki or solid conservative colored pair of slacks. Belt and shoes should be the same color, and socks should complement your shirt (or tie if you are wearing one). A sport coat is a nice final addition. If you need help with this, seek out the counsel of your wife, girlfriend, or mom.

Women: Business suits are the way to go. Skirts and dresses are difficult because you have to worry about length. Plunging necklines are a strict "no-no." Avoid the "busy" prints and stick with solid colors. Shoes should be sensible too. Don't rock those 5 inch heels at the interview.

For Both: Avoid colognes or perfumes. If you are worried about what you smell like wear an anti-perspirant. Many people are allergic to colognes and perfumes and the last thing you want them to remember about you is the fact you almost made their throat slam shut. Finally, keep jewelry to a minimum. You want your perspective employer to focus on you, not your bling.

Be Early, but not TOO Early

When you are given a specific time and place to meet, make sure you know exactly how to get there and how long it will take. I have been known to drive to the location the day before just so I am sure not to get lost. If you don't do that, at least you make sure to Mapquest the trip. Don't leave it up to your GPS system! I was an hour late foe a job interview because I relied solely on my GPS. Strangely enough, I didn't get that job.

If your interview begins at 7 pm, make sure you are there by 6:45 pm. Fifteen minutes is early enough to establish that you are excited about the job. Any earlier than that and you put your perspective employer in the position of having to pay attention to you before they may be ready to do so. You are there to prove that you will make life EASIER for them.

Study Your Future Church

If you are fortunate, the church will have a website. If you are very fortunate, the website will contain information about the history of the church, the area it serves, the staff, and the different ministries they provide. The more educated you can be about the church; the better you will sound in an interview. Instead of offering generalities, you may be able to insert a name or a specific ministry when answering a question. Your church will know that you are on the ball!

Send Follow-Up and Thank You Emails

It is always good practice to send a thank you email the day after the interview. In that email, make sure you make them aware that you are more than happy to answer any other questions that they may have. This usually generates a response. They may actually have questions or may just tell you that they don't. If you just say "Thank you" they may or may not respond. With any luck, the contact person will include some information about the next step of the process in the response as well. If you do not hear from them, it is acceptable to send a follow-up email within two weeks of your interview. Keep in mind that there is a lot to do and folks are probably doing it in their spare time! I was hired by a church who decided right after my interview that I was the one they wanted. Still, I had to wait weeks to hear about it! So, as my dad used to say, "Keep your pants on, you'll get your answer soon enough."

Always be Civil about Your Past Experiences

Even if your last boss blew up your house, ate your dog, and called your Mom fat, say positive things about them. You shouldn't lie, but there are things you can say that could be truthful. "My last boss helped me reevaluate my living environment." "My last boss enjoyed eating unique dishes" "My last boss took a real interest in my family." These positive things would be the truth. If you say negative things about your past employers, the church is more than justified in asking, "What horrible things will this person say about us?" If you have lapses in your resume or a lay-off to explain, be truthful. Tell them what you learned about your experience and make sure you include a reference letter that indicates the great stuff you did while you were there.

Last, but Certainly not the Least

Make sure that God is calling you to this position. You can only determine this by spending time in prayer. Ask God for guidance, wisdom, and strength in the process. If you feel any uncertainty in your spirit after you pray, the Holy Spirit may be telling you something. Listen to the Spirit! An open door or a job offer doesn't necessarily mean that this is the place God intended you to be in. If you put yourself in a job that God didn't intend for you it will assure two things. 1.

You aren't open to receive the blessings God has in store for you. 2. You are denying someone else the blessings that were intended for them.

13   Board (Bored) Meetings

Board meetings suck. There is absolutely no way around it. They are boring, usually inefficient, and sometimes mean-spirited. I've actually had long conversations about what color toilet paper the church should buy! (Surprisingly enough, there are people out there who care enough to argue about this for long periods of time.) If you are a paid ministry person, the board or staff meeting is inevitable.

I'll never forget the very first board meeting I attended at my second church. It was my second day on the job, and I had no idea what to expect. The meeting started at 7:00p.m. and my work day ended at 4p.m. I was commuting four hours every day. My family was still living in our old house, two hours away, waiting for its sale. Needless to say, I was already exhausted.

The meeting started with prayer. A very long sermon-type message from our esteemed board chairman. Then we moved on to my introduction. "Everyone, meet Jay, our new youth director." (I hate the term youth director, by the way.) Nothing but smiles, hugs, and handshakes. Things were definitely shaping up to be very positive. Next, we moved on to reviewing old business and accepting the meeting notes from the previous meeting. No snags so far.

We moved on to new business. First on the agenda was a discussion of tables for the Narthex (lobby, big room in the front of the church). The pastor felt like it was too crowded, and that we had ample room outside for the informational tables and such. This seemed like a logical argument to me, because the Narthex was very small. We had an ample courtyard, enough said. Except that it wasn't.

A woman on the board (who I will call "Mean Lady") proceeded to stand up and scream at our pastor. "You always make decisions like this without asking anyone!" "I've been to lots of other churches and all of them had better sermons and better activities." (What this had to do with tables in the Narthex I still don't know.) I'm sitting there thinking, "This lady has to be crazy; surely someone will stand up for our pastor."

Someone did indeed stand up to speak. However, instead of defending our pastor, he began to help "Mean Lady." By this time, I'm looking around for hidden cameras and I'm waiting for Dick Clark and Ed McMahon to come walking in. (I apologize to any of you who have no clue who those people are.)

Afterwards, my pastor approached me and asked how my first couple of days were going. He appeared as though nothing out of the ordinary had happened. "Um, terrific, right up until this board meeting," was my reply. "You'll get used to the way people get their points across around here," my pastor assured me. He was wrong. I never got used to it.

I've had great experiences and not-so-great experiences in church meetings. Usually, the difference lies in the attitudes of whoever is leading the meetings. My favorite people to work with have always been the types who don't allow disrespectful battles to occur. I also appreciate the leaders that have kept "side bar" discussions to a minimum. I appreciate when someone realizes that my time is valuable. In the same way, you should always remember that the time of others is equally as valuable. I've learned how to be a good meeting player:

1. **Don't talk to hear yourself talk.** Too many people feel the need to repeat something that doesn't need repeating

2. **This isn't "The Apprentice".** Treat people with God's love and patience. You're going to need the same one day.

3. **Provide your board leader with your points ahead of time.** Never spring anything on your board. It adds to the length of the meeting and it usually leads to uninformed discussions.

4. **Propose that everyone wear clown noses.** It's difficult to yell at someone if you both are wearing them.

Board meetings will never be fun, but you can get through them. If you nod off, just try not to get drool on the person sitting next to you.

14 How Dare They Say That About Me?

Not everyone will be totally enthralled with your decision to cover your students in Crisco and flour during your latest creative game. Sometimes, people will say things about you and your ministry that aren't all that nice. When criticism comes your way—and it most certainly will if you are doing what's necessary in youth ministry—you will have to cope with it. Does that sound easier said than done? Well yes, but it can be done.

Develop Thicker Skin

You are the perfect person for this youth ministry gig, because you care deeply about what people think. It's called vulnerability, and it's an absolute necessity in youth ministry. You have been called to be open and honest with the young people that are in your ministry. Sometimes, that means sharing your successes and failures with them in the hopes of teaching them about life. The same openness that attracts young people to you will also subject you to the possibility of being wounded.

I used the term "thicker skin" instead of "thick skin" for a reason. The last thing you want to do is create a stone wall around your heart. Sure, the stone wall may take away the possibility of being hurt, but it will also greatly diminish your ability to care enough about the people around you. If it sounds like these words come from experience, you are right.

My mother died while I was still in college. She was my sounding board and my biggest fan. My mom was always there when I needed her. When she died way too early from heart failure, I decided that hurting just wasn't for me. I decided that I wasn't going to let anyone get that close to me again.

It was a hard lesson to learn. It's still something that I have to combat. I'm just like you, I hate being wounded. Over the years, I have learned that I can't always protect myself from distress. I have also learned that thicker skin doesn't have to be as hard as stone.

Most criticism isn't personal. We have the astounding ability to weave it into a very personal tapestry, however. (At least I do.) I have learned to sit down and analyze criticism when it comes my way. I have realized that people usually have a problem with how you did it, and not with who you are.

Do Find Out Where the Criticism Comes From

A few years ago, I created a game that involved a kiddy pool filled with yellow–colored water, and a bag of bite sized chocolate–nutty candy bars. I called the game "Bobbing for Poo Poo", and I was sure that I was on the cutting edge of youth ministry brilliance. My kids LOVED it! It was one of the most hilarious moments in my youth ministry career. I went home knowing that I was, indeed, the man.

When I got home, there was a message on my home answering machine from an irate parent. She was horrified that I would play such a humiliating game with my students. She was partly right. (At least I didn't go with my original thought of using a brand new toilet instead of a kiddie pool!)

I called her the next day and she had calmed down a great deal. I apologized for playing such a gross game and told her that I wouldn't play it again. She started to cry and I asked the obvious question.

"What's wrong?"

After a lengthy conversation, I discovered that her husband was going through some serious medical issues, which had left him unable to work. She was working extra hours at her job, and taking on a second job. Come to find out, her criticism had very little to do with me or with "Bobbing for Poo Poo". She was going through some really tough stuff, and she couldn't express it to anyone else at the time. It happens.

When to Listen to Criticism

We aren't perfect. There will be times when your most brilliant ideas aren't really all that brilliant. It's important to have someone in your life that you can rely on to give you unbiased advice. It should be someone that you trust implicitly, and probably a person in ministry that has more experience than you. Obviously, you need to listen to the criticism that comes from your pastors, parents, and church board. They have your career in their hands and you don't want to ignore them. You have to decide, however, whether or not you're willing to fall on your sword in order to protect something you feel strongly about. A good church is going to be willing to let you take risks. With that in mind, it is never a good idea to put the health and safety of your youth group, and the church itself, in jeopardy.

Remember that You are a Christian!

One of the biggest joys of my life is that I am married to a talented and Godly woman who lives to use her gift of music for the church. For the most part, her involvement has been a blessing for me. There was one instance, however, that tested my heart.

My wife was in the middle of Praise Team practice when she discovered a mistake in some of the lyrics that appeared on the screen that the congregation would read to sing from. She approached our tech person to ask that the mistakes be corrected. The tech person must have been having a bad day because my wife received an uncalled for tongue lashing. At the conclusion of the practice, I walked into the sanctuary expecting to greet my normally cheerful wife. Instead I found out that she had been wounded. My first urge as a husband was to walk over to our tech person and punch him in the nose. Fortunately, the Holy Spirit spoke to me and reminded me that I had been called to be an example of Christian love. Believe me, the human side of my personality did not concur with the Holy Spirit. My wife could sense what I was thinking and she gently reminded me of the same things the Holy Spirit was trying to teach me. It is rarely easy, but we have to remember that we are Christians all the time.

If you hear the same criticism from more than one person who knows what they are talking about, heed it. At the very least, examine what they are saying closely. Look at what's being criticized and attempt to itemize it. Ask yourself the question, "Are these questions about my thought/plan/event valid?" If you can see the validity in the questions, then take the necessary measures to make your thought/plan/event even better.

15

If You Can't be in the Space You Love, Love the Space You're In

One Sunday, I was asked the most excellent question ever by a member of my church's finance team. "How would you like for us to double your salary?" (Yeah right!) No, instead he asked, "We can't figure out what to do with the old house on the property we purchased. We were going to plow it under for parking; do you think the youth could use it?"

That was the beginning of a yearlong odyssey that saw a very dedicated team of parents, teens, and church members convert an old run-down shack into an old run-down YOUTH shack!

We took out all of the walls, redid the floor with a garage floor coating, turned the kitchen into a snack bar complete with swing up/down bar, painted our youth group logo and other stuff on the wall in neon paint, hung black lights, and added two huge flat screen televisions, a karaoke machine, a vintage Atari video game system, an electronic dart board, and oh yes, a pool table.

We called it "The Spot", as in "This is THE SPOT for you." (Yeah it's corny, but it worked.) It became our youth group hang out. It had a cool little corner stage where I used to preach my lessons. We had kids in on Wednesday and Sunday nights for youth group meetings, and on Friday or Saturday nights for a late night hang out place. Kids could bring their friends who didn't know Jesus into a safe place where they could possibly become His best friend. It was pretty cool.

Things change and I don't work at that church any more. The space my new group occupies is also the "Traditional" sanctuary at the church. It has wooden pews, a baptismal and an old carpet. It's as far from "cool" as you can get. But it's the space we've been provided. The truth is that you have to utilize the space you have. If you have your own cool youth house or room, count yourself lucky. If you have to share space with other ministries and people in your church, count yourself in the majority.

What can you do to make that space all it can be? It's time to get creative!

Our kids used to see our sanctuary as kind of a scary mausoleum. When we first began to use it, they were not quite sure how to make the place their own. Luckily, I work for a very forward thinking church that views the church building as a ministry tool. On Wednesday nights, it becomes the youth building.

Warning: The Following Statements Might Cause Some Conservative Readers To Pop A Spleen!

We play games in the sanctuary. We eat pizza and drink soda in the sanctuary. We yell and tell really dumb jokes in the sanctuary. We run around in there, lie down on the pews, and generally have a really good time. We use it exactly the way I think Jesus intended us to use our house of worship. (We also learn about, pray to, cry out for, worship, and question God in there.)

Our church Narthex becomes our banquet hall. Our conference room becomes the place where middle schoolers hang out until their parents arrive to pick them up. Our parking lot turns into a football field afterwards. We use what we have, and as long as you're having the time of your life every week, it's a beautiful thing. (Quit griping!)

16 Wow, Adults in Your Church Can be Useful!

The formation of a youth support team is a very cool thing that I wish I could take credit for (I can't because my pastors came up with it). My support team is made up of parents, and members of our congregation, who simply love young people. They devote tons of time helping me with the logistical stuff, so that I can spend more time doing the fun stuff.

The purpose of my team is to provide support, ideas, friendly criticism, scheduling help, volunteers, and the all-important "responsible adult" angle to all of the crazy ideas I come up with. They are indispensable, and my biggest cheerleaders within our congregation. They make a point to talk to other members and help me tell them about all of the things we are doing. On more than one occasion, they have been able to hear the inevitable "church rumors" that happen from time to time, and provide people with the facts as they pertain to what we are all about. I can tell people about all of the cool stuff until I turn blue in the face, but when other respected people in your congregation can sing your group's praises, it adds instant credibility to your ministry.

Our youth team is all about communication. Communication is the thing that will help keep you and your ministry smelling minty fresh. Think about it. The people in your congregation are the ones who pay your salary and fund most of the activities of your youth group. It only stands to reason that they know exactly how their hard—.earned money is being spent.

There are so many things to consider when you are the one called to lead the youth ministry of your church. People expect dynamic results from you. My youth ministry team has been instrumental in the areas of:

Communication

We've mentioned talking to the congregation, but other methods are needed as well. My youth team handles things like phone calls to parents, creating special dinners and events to get the word out, and drumming up more help.

Promotions

I am constantly faced with finding new ways of telling the community about our ministry. One member of our team, for example, has taken the responsibility to create materials, contact our local paper, and prepare information tables at church on Sunday..

Fundraising

If you work at Saddleback or Willow Creek, you may not have to raise any money. I don't, so I do. I despise car washes and bake sales, so I found a person that has a knack for making money. We recently created a for—sale calendar that has all of our events for the year, crucial dates within the school calendar, and pictures of people in our youth group. We've discovered that people who don't have kids want to buy these things, just because it's a way of helping out.

The key is to find areas for people who don't necessarily want to work with teens, but still want to see your ministry succeed. If you have parents that want to get involved, but students that don't want to hang out with mom and dad on Wednesday nights, fundraising is one way to get that done.

I want to make one final recommendation about communication. If you haven't already been given the opportunity to get a little "face time" on Sunday mornings in front of the congregation, I suggest that you ask for it.

I am in charge of delivering the weekly announcements. During this time I get to lead off with a little bit about what our group is up to. (OK I lied, one more recommendation!) Ask your pastor for the opportunity to preach every once in awhile a while. Not only is it good experience, but it also proves to the rest of the congregation that you are exactly the talented, intelligent, thoughtful, and charismatic leader that your youth already know you are!

17   Parent Friendly

A major component of your youth ministry is typically overlooked. This component is every bit as important to the success of your ministry as formulating a great message, or coming up with a new way to utilize baloney and Skittles for your next game. I'm talking about parents! You know those folks who usually remain quiet until you really mess up? From now on, you are going to bring them into the picture.

Maybe you're thinking to yourself, "Yeah right, I've been there and done that." I know, I know, many parents' idea of youth group participation is dropping them off and picking them up. (Usually not on time, but beggars can't be choosers.) It's easy to blame them for viewing you as the free babysitter, or old what's his name at the church, but work with me for a minute. You can make them vital parts of your ministry.

Some of it is Our Fault!

You heard me right. I am going to blame some of the parental apathy directly on us youth minister folks. Far too many of us have labeled parents as lost causes. Many of us assume that parents aren't interested or don't care anyway. Why in the world should I waste my time on them? The answer to that is simple. If you want anything you do to stick, you need parents to reinforce it at home. I can hear you saying out loud now, "some of my parents aren't even Christians, how are they going to reinforce what I teach?" They want to, trust me on this.

Think about it. Why would a parent entrust their precious little babies to a person like you? Some of them haven't taken the time to get to know you at all. That must mean they don't care, right? WRONG! Parents do care. The bottom line is that they TRUST you! Even with all of the negative press about church, parents still believe in the positive message that you are teaching. It's a huge part of your job to help them reinforce it. Here's how:

Keep parents informed of what you are teaching their kids. A very simple way to keep parents informed is to create a website. The great news about websites today is that most web hosting companies make it easy to do. I use a great web host that only charges $70 a year. They even provide an easy to use program that lets you pick and choose a ton of options, from design to document downloading. Our website contains a blog that I update weekly with a brief synopsis of our message, upcoming event information, directions to the church, contact information, and our weekly dinner menu. (I don't include pictures of our youth. Too many predators online have ruined this option.)

Make Personal Contact. Make phone calls to your parents. The purpose of this call shouldn't be to discuss what a brat the kid is. Take a few moments to tell them how much you appreciate having their kids. Make a point to include specific instances where you have observed their children in moments of growth. You should also be actively searching for those parents that attend your church on Sundays, before and after the service. Shake their hands, give them hugs, and laugh with them. Always use these opportunities to build your relationship with them.

Visit Parents if They Are Open to It. I have served in churches that welcomed me into their homes like long lost family members. I have also served in churches that didn't at all appreciate the home visit. You know your parents (or at least you should). If you are going to go the home visit route, make sure that you call beforehand, so that you don't drop in at inappropriate times (e.g., dinner or Pilates time). At the end of your youth group night, make sure you have a few volunteers inside to watch your students. Then you can venture outside to greet those parents that do the drop off/pick up thing; and you can briefly express your gratitude for having their kids in your group.

Do Some Out of the Ordinary Stuff. As a youth minister, out of the ordinary is right in your wheelhouse. A ritual on the evening before the first day of school has become traditional for the families of my youth ministry. First, I purchase a load of inexpensive toys. Then I take a Sharpie pen and personalize a message on each toy. Finally, I drive around to each of my students' homes the night before the first day of school, and I put them on their doorstep. It's a lot of fun because you feel like you're doing something mischievous! For example, last year I bought a lot of plastic beach shovels. I personalized each one with their name, wrote a goofy message like, "I hope you DIG the first day of school!" Then I sign it and drop it off. When my students walk out of the door for that first nervous day, they have a reminder that I'm thinking about them. Out of all the efforts I make all year, this goofy activity gets one of the most positive responses. I have the feeling that if I didn't do it, my youth families would revolt

Organize a Parent's Night in Your Youth Room. Surprise parents and don't bombard them with information or requests to get involved. Simply open your room, let them play your games, feed them, and let them have a night of getting to know other parents. If you feel really inspired, provide them with a message that is designed specifically for them. Your parents will appreciate the opportunity to meet you on your home field. They will further appreciate that you view them as V.I.P's (Very Important Parents, sorry I couldn't resist the corny acronym). You can even put together a PowerPoint presentation with funny pics of their kids.

Go Out of Your Way to Get Your Safety Procedures Across. Parents want to know that their kids are safe. You can utilize that new website by posting your group rules. Also, make sure they understand that every volunteer has had a background check, and a thorough interview, by you. (You are doing that aren't you?) Seriously, if you haven't run a background check on your volunteers, you should right away. Unfortunately, we live in a world that makes this a necessity.

Pray For Them Daily. Prayer should be the backbone of your ministry. When you are on your knees with your eyes closed (or driving in your car with your eyes OPEN) take the opportunity to pray for your parents. You don't need to know their personal struggles. Just support their efforts to bring up their children. Every once in awhile, let your parents know that you are lifting them up in prayer.

I will make you this promise: if you commit to involve your parents, they will commit to being youth ministry-friendly. They may not volunteer in droves, and yes, some of them will still only pick up and drop off, but they will know that you have their children's best interests at heart. As a parent, I can assure you that it will be greatly appreciated.

18 Why Are We Doing That?

Chances are, many of you reading this are either new at your church, or getting ready to be new at another church. The pressure to be the "savior" is all too real and all too stressful. My good friend Jerry Gardner, a 20 year veteran of youth ministry, gave me some excellent advice about working with a new church: before making any major changes, spend a considerable amount of time (maybe even the first year if you have a really patient church) reviewing and observing the way things have already been done. This will give you the opportunity to see what works for your style of leadership, and what doesn't. It also helps you establish the fact that things won't be "my way or the highway."

There is, however, a fine line between being contemplative and being a weak leader. If some established tradition or event is not even close to your vision for the ministry, it should be removed. When you remove it, however, make sure that you clearly communicate exactly why it doesn't fit into your vision. Make sure you lay it out for your students, their parents, and your church leadership. Effectively communicating your vision is vital for the success of your new ministry.

Having said that, let me recommend that you put together a very concise written version of your vision, dreams, ideas, and plans for your group. Include everything, from the practical to the downright laughable. Even if everything you write down doesn't see the light of day, it will show people that you aren't afraid to think "outside of the box." They hired you for a reason. Undoubtedly, one of those reasons is that someone thinks you will be the one to lead the youth ministry to new heights.

If you put it down on paper, make sure that you are ready to explain exactly how and why it should be part of what you do. Never do anything simply to fill time. Everything you plan should have a purpose.

Holding a yearly series of Appreciative Inquiry meetings will help immensely with your vision planning. During Appreciative Inquiry, you look at the entire ministry, but you aren't picking on the negatives. In fact, saying "This stinks", or "What were you thinking?" isn't allowed. The goal is to focus on what your ministry did well, why it worked, and how you can make it happen in other areas. My favorite part of the process is when we talk about our goals for the future. It is wise to map out your year, and then talk about the years to come.

After you've talked about what you want to do, you need to set a time frame for getting it done. Nothing is more counterproductive than talking about what should be done without nailing it down. When you put a time frame on it, you've established a list of goals that you can point to anytime someone asks you the question, "What are you doing during the week?"

Each goal should outline one specific task. Let's say that you want your youth to serve breakfast at Sunday worship. That might encompass a number of things. Instead of simply saying, "We will begin serving breakfast on Sundays starting on July 10th", think about ALL of the steps that are required.

1. Put together a team that will cook (due June 1)

2. Find someone who is willing to shop for groceries (due June 6)

3. Decide on a menu (Due June 6)

4. Create an announcement for the church bulletin (Due June 13)

You get the point.

A great thing about planning is that you have the right to update it. You can add and subtract from it, based on your ministry needs and capabilities. Remember, sometimes things that were plausible in January turn out to be impossible in September. The process should work for you, and not the other way around.

19 Sadly, It Isn't All Fun and Games!

When you work closely with people, you are bound to experience amazing times of great joy and fun. Unfortunately, you are also bound to experience times of debilitating trauma and sadness. I am blessed to say that I have experienced many more times of joy, but I have also had to help others deal with some pretty crappy stuff.

Wade was a parent in one of my youth groups. He was definitely not the typical dad. He had raised his two boys by himself for most of their lives. He worked hard, rarely took time for himself, and loved his kids the best way he knew how. Sure, he was known to occasionally serve them rice crispy treats as a side dish at dinnertime. But the love was there, man.

Wade was an imposing figure. He was 6' 4" and well over 300 lbs. If you're a wrestling fan, imagine a friendlier version of King Kong Bundy. Now imagine King Kong Bundy who devoted nearly every second of his free time to serving God. This was an amazingly cool guy.

Wade's youngest son was in my youth group. Andrew is a lovable kid that would do just about anything in the world for you. Our youth group loves Andrew as much as a student could possibly be loved. I wish I had 100 Andrews.

A funny thing happened between Wade and me. We became friends. My wife and kids grew to love him like family. My daughter and son call him "Uncle Wade." I will always value his friendship because, honestly, friendships aren't easy to make in ministry. People usually have an agenda every time they speak to you. When you get the dinner invite, it's usually because someone wants to bend your ear about something that is going on (or should be going on) in church.

Advice Flash

When you get the opportunity to make real lasting friendships during your ministry jump all over them!

Wade became my right-hand man in youth ministry. He joined my youth support team and was there on Wednesday nights to help with the techie stuff or whatever else I needed. If I had an idea and needed it to be just a little crazier or fun, I could always bounce it off of Wade to get it done.

One day, Wade gave me some news that just didn't compute. He told me that he had cancer and that the doctors thought it was way too advanced to offer any real options. I certainly didn't like the news, but this was Wade. If anyone could beat something unbeatable, it was him.

Wade fought his illness far longer than any doctor realistically thought he could. Ultimately, my friend Wade got to meet his Lord. Now, as a Christian, I understand that my friend is experiencing the ultimate. I know that the pain and depression of his illness are long forgotten. I also know that his boys miss their father unbelievably. Sometimes, rather selfishly, I still wish my friend was here to make me laugh.

It's tough to help others to get through something that you are still grieving on. But helping young people cope with tough situations is part of the job description. It would be so much easier if I were just able to talk to Andrew on a professional level. To be able to reassure him that Jesus is holding him and that things will be all right.

Jesus is holding him, but life without your Dad is never all right. It just isn't. I've experienced the loss of both of my parents and it's never going to be all right. My experience as a Christian tells me that they are enjoying their heavenly existence like never before. My selfish, human side just hurts. It is OK to hurt right along with the people you minister to.

20 Signs of the Times: Surviving When You Lose Your Job

An entire book could be written with details of why youth ministry is a unique job. One area that is especially unique and difficult to fully understand is the way churches fund their various ministries. Churches typically rely on tithing, offerings, and other donations from their congregations and communities. As you might imagine, interchurch politics are ever-present. The question of how much money to spend where is ever-present.

Unfortunately, churches have to make tough decisions when it comes to finances just like any other business. The economic turmoil that the world has found itself in recently has hit the church hard. Many churches have had to make difficult decisions about staffing because money is hard to come by. Many churches have had to make tough choices about what to keep and what to do away with.

This is a topic that I can speak about with authority because I have experienced losing my job because of budget crunches not once, but twice over the past five years. Losing your job because you underperform is one thing, but it is especially tough to deal with when you lose it despite quality effort. If you are going through the same thing, take heart! God is still in control.

Don't Blame Yourself

When you lose your job the first question you are going to undoubtedly ask yourself is, "What could I have done to keep my job?" I agonized with this question both times. I spent a lot of time spilling over my attitude, my schedule, my effort, and professional adequacy. There were some particularly dark times when I even came to the conclusion that I must have not been cut out for this line of work. Sometimes life boils down to things that are beyond your control. Remember that God called you into youth ministry for a reason. You are good at what you do! Keep in mind that the big picture is often distorted by our inability to see it.

Adapt to the New Financial Climate

Adaptation isn't new to you because you are among the most creative creatures in the universe! How many times have you developed a new program with nothing more than an idea? How many times have you come up with a new hit game with nothing more than leftovers? Youth ministry professionals are experts when it comes to making something great out of very little. That means that you may have to create new ways to fund your ministry. It may even mean that you have to come up with ideas to supply some of the budget that pays your salary. I know it isn't the most appetizing of ideas. Believe me, I understand that you want don't want to focus another second on fundraising.

Maybe you won't have to. With any luck, there is a person or persons in your congregation with the gift of fundraising. Spend some time looking for that person. I have often found people in my congregations that would love to help your ministry succeed despite the fact that they may not have any desire at all to spend time with youth. The position of fundraiser is a perfect fit for those people.

Adapting to the new financial climate may ultimately mean that you have to scale back on your programming. You can do this effectively without sacrificing the quality of your ministry. Here are a few ideas.

Focus on your community's mission needs. Instead of planning a big-budget mission trip that requires a lot of money on travel, look a little closer to home. You can plan a life-changing mission trip without even leaving your town! Get in contact with churches in your area that have programs that benefit the community. Arrange for your group to spend the week sleeping on air mattresses in their fellowship hall. While you are there you can immerse your group completely into their mission efforts. Ask the youth minister of the church you are staying in to be your "guest speaker" for the week. You can even plan fun events with their youth group!

Take advantage of the free or next to free activities in your area. I live in South Florida, so the beach is a great resource to use. Your area has a number of things to do that your kids will love. If you live close to mountains plan a hiking trip. If you happen to have a minor league sports team in your town contact the team about group pricing for tickets. Plan a family picnic outside your youth room. Ask for the congregation to donate food and ask for your youth families to bring a dish!

Make your own food for youth events. Stop wasting money on delivery pizza! You can make six for the same amount it costs to buy one or two from the local pizza place. Your grocery store has readymade pizza crusts, inexpensive jars of pizza sauce, and the ingredients to make any pizza you can imagine. Plus, it's a lot more fun to create your own! Have a contest for the most original, best tasting, and worst tasting!

Share Resources- Staying up to date with training and the latest curriculum are expensive endeavors. Neither of these areas has to suffer if you do a little creative thinking. There are a number of great resources online that are free or nicely priced for youth ministry.

Free or Nearly Free Curriculum Sites

1. www.youthleaderscoach.com Jeanne Mayo is America's Youth Leader's Coach. She is an amazing youth pastor and an even better person! I have the honor of being involved in her mentoring group called *The Cadre.* Jeanne is known as "Mom" by most of the youth and adults she has mentored over her four decades in youth ministry. Her website has a great "freebies" section chocked full of useful stuff. I cannot say enough about this good woman of God.

2. www.youthpastor.com This site has some great readymade lessons that are available for free!

3. www.youthspecialties.com This is basically the everything site for youth ministry. Most of the things on this site are for sale, but they do offer some quality freebies. They also have an exhaustive listing of youth ministry positions that are looking to be filled across the country.

4. www.dougfields.com Mr. Fields is one of the most respected youth ministers around. His website offers great deals on his company's curriculum as well as an archive of freebies each month.

5. www.teenlifeministries.com This site offers what is called "The Zone" for youth leaders. Some of the things on the site are free, but if you can afford it, I recommend finding the $100 to sign up for their unlimited archives for a year. It will save you a ton of time in lesson planning and free you up to spend more time with your students.

Team Up When You Go to Conventions. Youth worker conventions are awesome opportunities to learn, network, and get away for a little while. Travel, hotel, and transportation can more than double the cost of the trip. Always call around and check to see if other youth workers in your area are also attending so that you can go along with them. Chipping in for gas and the cost of a van or car is a lot better than looking for airfare. Also, see if you can share a hotel room with other youth leaders. It's cost effective and a lot more fun too! You may also try calling churches in the area that may be able to help with housing. This is a long shot, but I've heard of it working before!

21 When Projects Become Larger than God

I want you to stop what you are doing right now and take a look at your calendar for the year. Don't just look at what is on the horizon, also look at the projects and events that have been accomplished already as well. What went into the planning process? To be more specific, how much of that process was God-inspired and how much was human?

You probably have at least one event on your calendar that has become tradition at your church. Something you do every year that energizes the congregation, makes your parents and youth buzz with excitement, and gives you more headaches than you care to acknowledge. Maybe this event or project is way beyond the point where anyone is asking the question, "Why are we doing this?" If you have one or more of these types of things on your calendar you might be in danger of doing something you never wanted to do in your ministry career. You might be making a project bigger than God.

I can hear you saying now, "The Rhubarb Pie Fundraiser brings our church together in so many wonderful ways! We gather all generations together and accomplish great things for the Kingdom!" Believe me, I understand. The church does a great job of rallying around big events. It gives us a sense of purpose and accomplishment when we come together to do something big. And, if some people get ministered to, or we raise a lot of money for our ministries, then it must have been o.k. with God. Right?

I've worked hard at several big projects in my life. I've devoted huge amounts of energy and time to things that helped my church. I've enjoyed the pats on the back and the congratulations that came after the big efforts. Sadly, I've even created my share of projects that became "church tradition". These projects will always be done the same way, at the same time, year after year without ever being questioned or rethought. No need to mess with success!

Except, I think there is. The older I become, the more I am looking at what success means. It used to mean huge numbers, state-of-the-art presentations, and a lot of flash. I wanted to speak messages that led students to the altar in huge waves. I did it all for the Lord, or I used to say I did anyway. The truth is that I did a lot of it for me. I did a lot of it for the gratification of being noticed and thanked. Once the event was over, it was time to move on to the next one. Bigger and better, all the time.

Is bigger and better creating narrow and shallow? We will never eliminate the need for fundraisers and events in youth ministry. I love the good folks who claim to do nothing but open their doors for small group time and thousands of Jesus-starved teens come rushing through their doors. They have the answers and talent that I simply do not possess. For the rest of us, the ultra time consuming once a year event is going to be on the schedule at least once, if not a few times each year. How do we do it well without making it the sole focus of what we do?

Do the Important Stuff Just as Well

Don't skimp on Sunday school lessons or midweek Bible studies. Give them just as much effort as you do planning the Huge Rhubarb Pie Sale. I know, thousands of people and tons of money are raised with the pie sale and eight kids show up to Sunday school. Which will produce the eternal results that really matter? When you are lying in the pine box wearing the makeup that makes you look like a dead circus clown do you want to be known as the guy or gal who broke the rhubarb sales record or the guy or gal who helped lead a young person to the Lord?

Research the Climate of the Great Event

If you are going to take the stand that eliminates one of the great traditional events in your church make sure you know who is on your side. How does your Senior Pastor feel about the decision? How do your parents feel about the decision? Are you willing to fall on your sword over eliminating the time honored event? Chances are great that eliminating an event that has become part of the identity of a church or a youth group is going to be unpopular with some folks. You can expect nasty e-mails, phone calls, or looks waiting for you at every turn. Those are from the people who are brave enough to make their feelings known by you. Be aware of the sniper in the grassy knoll who just got through patting you on the back. The church is not a place that typically accepts change well.

That doesn't mean that you shouldn't make those changes, however. Some huge dinosaur events deserve to be slaughtered. I know there are colossal time and money eating events on youth group calendars all over this world just because no one has the courage to ask, "Is this still working for us?" If you've done your research, prayed it through, and haven't received a good answer for "Why?" then it's time to end the Rhubarb Pie Sale. Just make sure you are ready to explain it to the good folks who will be expecting an answer.

22 A Completely Absurd Message for the Whole Church

A guy went to the doctor's office with a horrible headache. Not just the normal "My head sorta tingles a little bit" type of headache, but the kind that feels like someone has been hitting you with a hammer wrapped in barbed wire. After the doctor did a brief examination, he asked the man a simple question. "Do your headaches typically start after any specific activity?" The man answered, "Yes, they usually begin shortly after I begin hitting myself in the head with this hammer!"

The doctor wrote the man a prescription that read, "After each hammer pounding, take a long brisk walk, followed by an hour of yoga." The man followed the doctor's advice precisely. After several months, he returned to the doctor's office with the same horrible headaches.

The doctor scratched his chin and began to ponder the man's condition. After thinking about it for a little while, he wrote the man a new prescription. "After each head pounding, pour a bag of thumbtacks onto the floor and sit on them completely naked."

The man followed the new advice for a couple of months and returned to the doctor's office without finding any relief. Not only were the headaches not going away, but now his buttocks were often sore and irritated. The man was puzzled by his condition, for he was dutifully following the advice of his doctor.

Lots of churches have difficulty attracting certain segments of the population. Some churches struggle with getting "young people" into the church, others need to attract more men, and others want midgets from upper Mongolia. How do we go about attracting those folks we need to reach?

We usually start with an event. A group of terrific people get together and form a planning committee. "If we want to tap into the Upper Mongolia midget market, we need to offer what those wonderfully short Mongolians are looking for!" How about a one–time festival with the third best Mongolian band in the county, and some frozen delights straight from the nearby bulk food warehouse? That should do the trick.

Now we need to get the word out. What's the best way to reach vertically challenged Upper Mongolians? Advertise the event on the local Portuguese radio station, of course! What's that you say? Do Mongolians listen to Portuguese radio? Well, they should if they don't! WE listen to Portuguese radio, and it's just dandy. And don't we really want midget Upper Mongolians who speak Portuguese anyway?

So we have the planning committee, the third best Mongolian band in the county, lots of frozen delights, and we have advertised the event on local Portuguese radio. Now, all we have to do is wait for hordes of new folks to arrive.

Except they don't. Mostly, Portuguese people of average height showed up, and we already have a bunch of those folks. Besides, most of those Portuguese people already go to the mega church, "Our step-sister of Portuguese Descent", down the street. They have shown up merely to eat our pastry puffs, and listen to "Genghis and the Khan-ibals" until it was time to go home. We did have two kinda short Lower Mongolians show up, but they weren't what we were looking for. And we ran out of brochures anyway.

The next week at the follow-up meeting, the planning committee begins to go pour over the details of the event. Let's start positive!

- Genghis and the Khan-ibals rocked the house, baby!

- We have plenty of pastry puffs left over; we can serve them for months at various events.

- We have oodles of great pictures for next month's newsletter.

- We gave out ALL of our brochures!

Ok, Ok, what should we do differently next year? Nothing? You betcha! That was a great event!

My examples are ridiculous, of course. What do long walks, yoga, and sitting on thumbtacks have to do with ending headaches? Just a thought, but *stop hitting yourself in the head with the hammer!* And as far as reaching midget Upper Mongolians goes...maybe we should try shorter sermons (insert rim shot here.)

As preposterous as all of that sounds, a lot of churches do exactly the same type of stuff, week after week. We need more kids, so we have an event with dunk tanks and clowns. We advertise the event, aimed at introducing NEW people to God, on the local Christian station. And we do all of this to invite kids to a church that probably isn't ready for kids to come to it! All because someone said, "What can we do to get more kids to our church?"

The people you want to attract don't shy away from your church because you haven't had enough one–time events. They shy away because your church doesn't have what they are looking for. Or maybe they don't know that your church exists. Here's a wild idea... maybe your church isn't supposed to be all things to all people. If you don't have a single midget from Upper Mongolia in your community, then you probably don't need to book Genghis and the Khan-ibals any time soon.

But if your church is smack dab in the middle of lit-tle–kid land, and you don't have a single person under the age of 87 in the church, it's time to look around and do some thinking. Is that pipe organ still reaching the hearts of those young people in your community? Are those stained glass windows still screaming, "We are all about you!" to those young-ins? Maybe it's time to put those tried and true church symbols away for a little bit and try something a bit more "Groovy, hip, with-it, and rad."

PART III

Your Body is a Temple, Start Treating it that way!

"Physical training is good, but training for godliness is much better, promising benefits in this life and in the life to come."

1 Timothy 4:8 (*NLT*)

23 Physical Health and Your Ministry

I am, by no means, a Licensed Nutritionist. Nor am I a certified personal trainer. I am simply a kinda chubby guy who used to be a really chubby guy. The lifestyle of a youth minister can add unwanted pounds to anyone. Think about it, we spend hours upon hours with teenagers who typically eat as if Reese's was one of the major food groups. We spend a lot of time on the road, where conscientious and economically sound choices for food usually involves a window and a menu screen you talk into. It's difficult to be in shape. (Yes, I know, *round* is a shape!)

Before you throw this book down in disgust, let me assure you of one thing. This isn't going to be a "tsk tsk...you undisciplined slob" type of thing. You're either thinking about youth ministry, or you are currently involved. The last thing anyone could ever accuse you of is laziness. I know how dedicated you are, how tireless are your efforts, and how totally devoted you are to God and others. Grant me the permission to ask you to be totally devoted to one more person: yourself.

I know the Bible tells us to put others before ourselves. But sometimes we make the mistake of thinking that it's sinful to care about ourselves. It's not. In fact, I want you to start thinking about nutrition and exercise as a real form of worship to the God you love. The vessels we occupy are beautiful and complex. You are the hands and feet of God.

Day after day, you push yourself to mental, emotional, and physical exhaustion. You have been called to lead a transformation in the spiritual lives of people who mostly want to leave messages on Facebook. The task is enormous, and the strain it puts on your health can be even greater. Let's talk about how much effort we put into ourselves.

Eating well doesn't have to be torture. I spent most of my life thinking it was. I used that as an excuse to treat myself to anything greasy and cheesy. (I'm not perfect; sometimes I still succumb to greasy and cheesy.) Every day, I have to make the choice to put rocket fuel into my body.

Let's get this out of the way. "Fad" diets work for the short term. There are lots of plans out there that claim quick results in just a few weeks. Sure, they work for a little while. But what happens when you reach the weight goal you set for yourself at the beginning? If you are like me, you celebrate by putting on more weight than you had before you started.

Let's begin to look at health from a different point of view. Instead of a weight loss goal, let's set our goal as "the level of health that will help me minister to my youth at an optimal level." That will probably be a different level for everyone. Some of us need to shed a few pounds so that we can participate in the physical activities that we plan for our youth. Some of us need to lower our blood pressure so that we can have the extra energy we need to remain vital. Whatever your level is, you can find it with a few long-term changes.

Rule #1: Don't Starve Yourself!

Your body needs calories to work properly. You wouldn't solve poor performance in your car by giving it less gas, would you? Of course not. By that same logic, you should never deny your body its needed fuel. If you are an average sized active male, you need at least 2,000 calories per day. You can get those calories in one meal from McDonalds, or you can get more than enough to eat throughout the day by eating smarter. Begin to think of foods like lean poultry, beef, pork, lamb, and game. These foods are packed with the protein your muscles need to thrive. Carbohydrates have received an awful blemish in some dietary circles. Some carbs deserve the rap, like products made with white flours. These include white breads, pastas, cakes, doughnuts, cookies, etc. However, whole grain carbohydrates are amazing for your body. They provide much needed fiber and they help you feel fuller, longer.

I know that lots of people hate their veggies! For most of my life, I was one of those people. Then I got brave and started to add them to my cooking. I found out that not only did I like most vegetables, I actually found myself craving them throughout the day. I even began taking a green drink in the morning that is packed with vitamins and nutrients, which helps me to get going.

A word of warning about green drinks: lots of them taste like grass clippings. I found one that I can stand. I won't lie and tell you it's better than a chocolate milkshake. I look at it like confession. It's not my favorite thing, but it's essential to my health. My greens drink is one thing I can point to in my diet that I can honestly say adds something significant to my energy level.

Eating well will also keep you in the game. Sure, it prolongs your life and all of that jazz. But it also keeps those pesky little colds away as well. How many different kids are you exposed to on a weekly basis? Now think about how many kids your kids are exposed to on a weekly basis. Do some multiplication and we are talking about a lot of exposure to germs. Eating well will definitely reduce the amount of sick days you have to take. I speak from experience — I can't remember the last time I had any kind of serious cold.

Repeat after me...I will try my hardest to LOVE salad! Say it again just in case you need convincing. Salads are among the most versatile and easy things you can eat. You don't have to be Emeril Lagasse to concoct a good salad. (Potato salad doesn't count.) Start with a good base of greens. I suggest romaine or a spring mix of bagged greens from your grocery store. Add things like mushrooms, beans, peppers, tomatoes, broccoli, squash, zucchini, boiled egg, a little reduced–fat shredded cheese, and some lean meat or tuna. You can even use the tasty dressings if you follow one little hint: never pour it directly on your salad. Instead, pour some to the side and stick the tines of your fork in it lightly before each bite. You will get plenty of flavor, and not use nearly as much dressing as you used to.

Rule #2: Treat Yourself Every Once In A While!

I know a lot of the dietary gurus would read this and shudder with disgust. But every once in a while, maybe even once a week, eat something that you really love. If you love pizza, have a slice or two. If you are a dessert person, have a sundae or a slice of cheese cake. Just remember to get back to eating the really good stuff for

95% of your week. If you do that, your little "cheat" meals will actually serve as a rev start for your metabolism! (If you don't believe me look it up!) It's like a little reward for treating yourself right. I look forward all week to my moment of culinary debauchery.

Rule #3: Eat Five or Six Small Meals throughout the Day

Eating many small meals throughout the day is time consuming and requires some planning. But if you give your body smaller portions, your metabolism will remain stoked like a fire throughout the day. Cramming three large meals into the body requires a lot of energy to convert it into the stuff we need. A lot of times our body isn't through converting the previous meal when we add another huge one to the pile. When we eat a few big meals a day, our metabolism starts and stops. On the other hand, five or six smaller portions throughout the day places much less of a burden on our system. It tells our metabolism that it's going to have to work all day long. It's like putting branches into a wood chipper. If you try to cram the whole trunk in at one time, it will eventually get bogged down and stop. If you add small branches a little at a time, however, the chipper will keep running at optimal speed.

Rule #4: Drink Plenty of Water

Sometimes, the feeling of thirst is misread as hunger. The recommended amount of water is 8–8oz. glasses per day. This sounds like a lot, and it is. But if you keep a water bottle on your desk at all times, you can sip away and get what your body needs without a problem.

Rule #5: Take a Multivitamin Every Day

There are a variety of good, inexpensive brands out there. I have read a lot about One-A-Day Men's Health Formula, which is packed full of what you need. It's what I take, and it's hard to find a better vitamin for the money.

Rule #6: Look In the Freezer Section

Frozen meals can actually be a great choice. Understand that I'm not talking about Hungry Man XXXL or anything like that. Look for brands like Kashi, South Beach Diet, Lean Cuisine, and Healthy Choice. These meals are portioned correctly, are very tasty, and offer a good sample of many of the food groups. One word of warning—if you are sodium sensitive, make sure you pick ones that are lower in sodium.

Frozen fruits and vegetables are also good choices for the youth minister. They are economical, store easily, and are usually just as healthful as fresh. They have the added bonus of longer shelf life. As with anything else, make sure you read the labels. Some frozen vegetables contain added salts and fats. Make sure you buy products that contain only the vegetables you are looking for.

Rule #7: Use Nonstick Cookware and Cooking Sprays

Avoid a lot of unnecessary calories and fats by using non–stick cookware and cooking sprays. A good non-stick piece of cookware will allow you to sauté meats and vegetables without adding anything. When you do need moisture, try using a little water or cooking spray. These will do the job without adding any extra calories.

Rule #8: A Little Fat Is a Good Thing

Fat is a word that seems to have a negative connotation, but some fat in your diet is absolutely necessary. We should all listen to the current advice that is out there, however. Stay away from trans-fats and saturated fats. Instead, supplement your diet with things like olive oil, omega 3 fatty acids (salmon is an excellent source), and flaxseed oils.

Rule #9: Eat To Live, Don't Live To Eat

There are so many more important things than food to find pleasure in! Don't treat meals as though they are your primary fun activities for the day. It's perfectly fine to look forward to spending time with loved ones at the kitchen table, but it's sad when we look forward to gorging ourselves on stuff that isn't good for us. I think you will find that the good times we usually associate with food are actually good times because of the people we eat the food with.

Rule #10: Don't Beat Yourself Up For Slipping Up

So what, you had a moment and you ate half a pizza. Don't consider yourself an absolute failure. This only leads to a defeated attitude towards eating. Sometimes, stress or a lack of time makes us do crazy stuff. If it happens, wipe your mouth and get right back on the healthy horse. Trust me, it's gonna be all right.

24 Exercise More Than Those Demons

Spending time with God, being a professional, and eating well are not the only characteristics of the healthy youth minister. Physical exercise is also essential to the overall healthy picture. Now, before you are again tempted to put this book down, resist the urge and keep reading!

Exercise doesn't have to be miserable. If you have attempted to exercise in the past and absolutely hated it, you simply didn't find the right activity for you. There are countless ways to break a sweat that can actually turn out to be a good time.

My wife teaches high school and they offer a "Zumba" class after hours. Zumba is mix of different dances that she swears is loads of fun. I was able to watch it for about a zillionth of a nanosecond before deciding that it wasn't for me. That happens to be one of the beauties of exercise, however. Different strokes for different folks.

The key is to find something that doesn't feel like work. If watching Rocky gets you pumped up, try taking a kenpo class. Kenpo is a mix of kicks and punches that will burn a ton of calories. If you don't have the money or ambition to take part in a formalized class, try shadow boxing for a set amount of time. Try to do a little bit more each time before resting, and before you know it, you'll be ready to go a few rounds with Clubber

Lang. (Don't take this literally, however, or you will probably get your butt kicked!)

Maybe punching and kicking isn't your thing. If not, try to make a little time in your day for a walk. Every time you do it, try to increase the pace just a bit. Always remember to listen to your body. If you feel unusual discomfort, tightness in the chest, tingling, or anything else that isn't quite kosher, stop immediately. It's a good idea to consult a physician before you start an exercise program, if it's something you haven't done in a while. Start slow and don't feel like you are competing with anyone. You aren't trying to make the Olympic long-distance running team.

I like to lift weights. I'm not, nor will I ever be, a Greek god. It's simply a fun way for me to burn off stress and a few calories. When I started out, I found a nearby park with a nice little fitness room. They offer a year's membership for a hundred bucks. There are times during the year when I hit the gym 5 or 6 days a week. There are also times when I have hit McDonalds with more frequency than the gym. The key is, do what you can do. Don't beat yourself up if you can't find the time or energy to hit the gym. (And don't do the McDonalds thing, just drive by and give the window attendant a friendly wave.)

A common misconception of some females is that they shouldn't lift weights for fear of becoming "bulky", or looking too masculine. It isn't going to happen. Most of the women who appear in bodybuilding magazines are putting more into their bodies than simple protein powders and Gatorade (if you catch my drift). Ladies, remember that you don't have the testosterone levels of the typical male. Therefore, your weight training won't result in Incredible Hulk muscles. You will gain more confidence and the incredible feeling of doing something wonderful for yourself!

This Part Is For Married Readers Only!

Most books in the Christian reading section probably won't mention this exercise benefit. [Exercise gives you stamina and energy for the times after the little ones go to bed. It makes sense. Exercise increases your capacity for prolonged activity, proper breathing, and self-confidence. If we feel and look better physically, it only stands to reason that "the fun times" will happen with more frequency! (Can I get an "AMEN", brothers and sisters?

25 How to Eat Healthy at the Fast Food Joint

There will be times as a youth minister when you will have to eat on the road. While this isn't the ideal thing to do on a regular basis if you want to live a long and healthy life, it is practically part of the job description. Below I have listed a pretty good group of fast food places and some options that are less than 300 calories. Understand that menus do change and these places update their nutritional information from time to time. Order the stuff that isn't too bad, and you won't have to carry along carrot sticks while the rest of your group chews, burps, and smiles.

Quick Nutrition Facts at Your Group's Favorite Places (in Alphabetical Order)

Arbys

Menu Item	Cal.	Fat (g)	Chol (mg)	NA (mg)	Pro. (g)
Martha's Vineyard Salad	272	9	61	609	22
Grilled Santa Fe Salad	279	10	61	679	25
Ham/Swiss Melt	300	8	35	1070	18

Burger King

Hamburger	260	10	35	490	13
Cheeseburger	300	14	45	710	16
Whopper Jr.	260	14	35	440	13
Spicy Chick'n Crisp (no mayo)	300	12	20	1450	12
Chicken Tenders	270	16	45	460	14
Chicken Fries (6 piece)	250	15	30	820	14
Fries (value menu size)	220	11	0	340	2
Onion rings (value menu size)	260	10	35	480	13
Mozzarella Sticks (4 piece)	280	15	35	650	11
Croissan'wich (egg/cheese)	300	16	180	690	11
Breakfast Burrito (Bac/egg/ch/salsa)	300	16	145	910	15

Dairy Queen

Hot Dog	290	7	35	900	11
Crispy Chicken Wrap	290	17	30	620	11
Grilled Chicken Wrap	200	13	35	450	12
Crispy Chicken Flame Thrower Wrap	300	18	35	620	11

HEALTHIER OPTIONS ARE IN BOLDFACE

Del Taco

Menu Item	Cal	Fat (g)	Chol (mg)	NA (mg)	Pro (g)
Taco	130	7	20	180	7
Soft Taco	150	6	20	330	8
Chicken Soft Taco	220	12	45	490	12
Crispy Fish Taco	300	17	25	330	8
Shredded Beef Taco Del Carbon	200	10	30	280	11
Steak Taco Del Carbon	210	8	30	410	9
Chicken Taco Del Carbon	150	5	30	300	9
Carne Asada Taco	230	10	30	480	10
Macho Taco	300	17	70	630	20
Sante Fe Chicken Soft Taco	240	12	40	450	12
Breakfast Del Carbon Taco	140	5	135	170	7
Hash Brown Sticks (5 piece)	210	15	0	180	0
Fries (small)	270	16	0	310	3

Hardees

Menu Item	Cal.	Fat g.	Chol . mg	NA mg	Pro. g
Cinnamon 'n' Raisin Biscuit	300	15	0	680	3
Pancakes (3 cakes)	300	5	25	830	8
Hash Rounds (small)	250	16	0	360	3
Side Salad	120	7	20	160	7
Fried Chicken leg	170	7	45	570	13
Cole Slaw (small)	170	10	10	140	1
Mashed Potatoes (small)	90	2	0	410	1

HEALTHIER OPTIONS ARE IN BOLDFACE

Jack In The Box

Menu Item	Cal.	Fat (g)	Chol. (mg)	Sod. (mg)	Pro (g)
Hamburger	290	12	30	570	14
Grilled Chicken Strips (4)	240	6	115	1060	43
Beef Monster Taco	240	14	20	390	8
Beef Taco (regular)	180	10	10	270	6
Grilled Chicken Salad	240	8	70	650	28
Side Salad	50	3	10	65	2
Spicy Corn Sticks	140	7	0	140	2
Egg Roll	150	7	5	320	5
Fries (small)	290	13	0	530	3
Cheese Sticks (small)	280	16	25	590	12
Breakfast Jack	280	11	240	790	16

Kentucky Fried Chicken

	Cal.	Fat	Chol.	Sod.	Pro
Grilled Caesar Salad	210	7	85	1030	28
Grilled BLT Salad	230	8	90	920	34
KFC Snacker (Honey BBQ)	210	3	35	470	13
Crispy Strips (2 Piece)	230	11	70	1280	33
Grilled Fillet	140	3	70	560	26
Original Fillet	170	7	55	360	23
Toasted Crispy Strip Wrap*	280	10	35	820	17
Toasted Tender Grill Wrap*	240	8	50	630	20
Toasted Grilled Wrap*	240	8	45	680	19
Mini Melt	250	7	45	690	15
Grilled Fillet Sandwich*	290	4.5	70	720	32
Gizzards	200	11	100	800	11
Livers	180	10	200	620	11
* = NO SAUCE	**All Grilled Chicken Pieces Are Under 300 Calories**				

Krystal

Menu Item	Cal	Fat (g)	Chol. (mg)	Sod. (mg)	Pro g
Krystal	130	6	15	330	6
Cheese Krystal	160	8	20	470	7
Bacon/Cheese Krystal	200	11	30	580	8
Double Krystal	290	13	35	580	12
Kryspers	150	7	5	270	1
Chili Cheese Krystal	290	19	50	670	15
Chik'n Bites (small)	200	7	35	690	15
Biscuits and Gravy	280	14	0	710	5
Krystal Sunriser	200	11	115	620	11
Corn Pups	240	14	30	520	5
Chili Cheese Pup	230	14	35	560	11
Plain Pup	150	8	20	450	6
Chili (large)	300	11	25	200	17
Chicken Bites Salad	290	20	65	490	20
Krystal Chik	300	16	35	800	14
Egg on Toast	230	9	190	580	12
Sausage on Toast	300	20	30	420	9
Pancakes (4 cakes)	280	8	20	560	7

Long John Silver's

Menu Item	Cal	Fat (g)	Chol. (mg)	Sod. (mg)	Pro g
Battered Fish (1piece)	260	16	35	790	12
Battered Shrimp (3 piece)	130	9	45	480	5
Popcorn Shrimp Snack	270	16	75	570	9
Lobster Bites Snack	230	9	60	520	9
Crispy Breaded Whitefish	190	10	20	540	9
Grilled Pacific Salmon (2) 150	5	50	440	24	
Grilled Talapia	110	2.5	55	250	22

Long John Silver's Continued

Menu Item	Cal	Fat (g)	Chol. (mg)	Sod (mg)	pro g
Shrimp Scampi (8 pieces)	200	13	135	650	17
Chicken Plank (1)	140	8	20	480	8
Freshside Grille Smart-choice Salmon	280	7	50	1010	27
Freshside Grille Smart-choice Talapia	250	4.5	60	820	25
Golden Fries (small)	230	2.5	0	350	3

McDonalds

Menu Item	Cal.	Fat g.	Chol. mg	Sod. mg	Pro. g
Hamburger	250	9	25	520	12
Ranch Grilled Snack Wrap	270	10	45	830	18
Honey Mustard Grilled Snack Wrap	260	9	45	800	18
Chipolte Grilled Snack Wrap	260	9	45	830	18
Cheeseburger	300	12	40	750	15
Southwest Salad (no chicken)	140	4.5	10	150	6
Bacon Ranch Salad (with chicken)	260	9	90	1010	33
Chicken McNuggets (6 pieces)	280	17	40	600	14
Fruit and Yogurt Parfait (with granola)	160	2	5	85	4
Egg McMuffin	300	12	260	820	18
Sausage Burrito	300	16	115	830	12
Fruit and Maple Oatmeal	290	4.5	10	160	5

HEALTHIER OPTIONS ARE IN BOLDFACE

Popeye's

Menu Item	Cal	Fat (g)	Chol. (mg)	Sod (mg)	pro g
Louisiana Travelers Nuggets (6 piece)	220	12	40	500	15
Naked Chicken Strips (3 strips)	220	10	80	720	30
Popcorn Shrimp	280	16	95	1110	12
Chicken Sausage Jamba-laya	220	11	32	760	10
Smothered Chicken	210	8	23	743	10
Chicken Etouffee (regu-lar)	160	10	20	870	12
Crawfish Etouffee (regu-lar)	180	5	48	640	7

Sonic

Menu Item	Cal.	Fat g.	Chol. mg	Sod. mg	Pro. g
Corn Dog	210	11	20	530	6
Grilled Chicken Salad	250	10	100	1070	29
French Fries (small)	200	8	0	270	2
Ched 'R' Bites (12 pieces)	280	15	30	740	13

HEALTHIER OPTIONS ARE IN BOLDFACE

Subway

6 inch sub w/ lettuce, tomato, onions, green peppers, pickles, and olives with meats mentioned below

Menu Item	Cal.	Fat g.	Chol. mg	Sod. mg	Pro. g
Ham	290	4.5	25	1200	18
Turkey	280	5	15	900	19
Turkey and Ham	300	4	25	1140	19
Veggie Delite	230	2.5	0	410	8
Mini Subs					
Ham	180	2.5	10	670	10
Roast Beef	200	3	15	480	15
Turkey	190	2.5	15	610	12
All salads on the 6 grams of Fat or less menu are no more than...	200	3.5	50	850	20
All soups other than chili are no more than	290	13	50	990	20
All egg muffin melts are under 300 calories except for the "Mega Muffin"					

HEALTHIER OPTIONS ARE IN BOLDFACE

Taco Bell

Menu Item	Cal.	Fat g	Chol. mg	Sod. mg	Pro g.
Crunchy Taco (fresco)	150	7	20	350	8
Soft Taco (fresco)	190	7	20	580	8
Chicken Soft Taco (fresco)	170	4	25	680	12
Steak Grilled Soft Taco (fresco)	160	6	15	550	9
Nacho Cheese Beef Gordita	290	14	20	720	12
Nacho Cheese Chicken Gordita	270	10	25	760	15
Nacho Cheese Steak Gordita	260	11	15	690	12
Beef Gordita Supreme	300	13	35	500	13
Chicken Gordita Supreme	270	10	35	630	17
Steak Gordita Supreme	270	11	30	550	14
Cheesy Nachos	280	17	0	300	4
Cheese Rollup	200	10	20	480	9
Chicken Flatbread Sandwich	290	15	35	720	15
Mini Quesadilla	190	9	20	450	9
Tostada	250	10	25	730	11

HEALTHIER OPTIONS ARE IN BOLDFACE

Wendy's

All premium salads are under 300 calories if you order "1/2 Size"

Menu Item	Cal.	Fat g.	Chol. mg	Sod. mg	Pro. g
Small Chili	220	7	35	870	18
Jr. Hamburger	230	8	30	480	12
Chicken Nuggets (5 piece)	230	14	35	430	12
Grilled Chicken Wrap	260	10	55	750	20
Natural Cut Fries (value size)	220	11	0	270	3

White Castle

Menu Item	Cal.	Fat g.	Chol. mg	Sod. mg	Pro. g
Original Slider	140	6	10	360	7
Cheese Burger	170	9	15	550	8
Jalapeno Cheese Burger	160	9	20	460	9
Bacon Cheese Burger	190	11	20	550	9
Pulled Pork Slider	170	4.5	25	460	9
Double Original	240	12	20	660	12
Double W/ Cheese	300	17	30	940	15
Double Jalapeno W/ Cheese	280	17	30	860	15
All Breakfast Sliders except Sausage, egg, cheese, and Huevos Ranchero) are under 300 Calories.					

HEALTHIER OPTIONS ARE IN BOLDFACE

Nutritional Information Reference

Fast food menu web information as of January, 2011

Arbys:
www.arbys.com/nutrition/Arbys_Nutrition_Website.pdf
Burger King:
www.bk.com/cms/en/us/cms_out/digital_assets/files/pages/NutritionInformation.pdf
Dairy Queen:
www.dairyqueen.com/upload/DQFoodandTreatNutritionBrochure.pdf
Del Taco:
www.deltaco.com/nutrition.html
Hardees:
www.hardees.com/system/pdf_menus/9/original/Hardees_Nutritionals_5.20.10.pdf?1285096241
Jack in the box:
www.jackinthebox.com/pdf/NutritionalGuide_2010.pdf
KFC:
www.kfc.com/nutrition/pdf/kfc_nutrition.pdf
Krystal:
krystal.com/wp-con-tent/themes/krystal/pdf/NutritionalInformation.pdf
Long John Silver's:
www.longjohnsilvers.com/pdf/LJS_Nutritional_Information.pdf

McDonalds:
http://nutrition.mcdonalds.com/nutritionexchange/
nutritionfacts.pdf
Popeyes:
www.popeyes.com/nutrition.pdf
Sonic:
www.sonicdrivein.com/pdfs/menu/SonicNutritionGu
ide.pdf
Subway:
www.subway.com/applications/NutritionInfo/nutriti
onlist.aspx?id=sandwich
Taco Bell:
www.tacobell.com/nutrition/information
Wendy's:
www.wendys.com/food/pdf/us/nutrition.pdf
White Castle:
www.whitecastle.com/system/blocks/data/6/origina
l/System_Nutritional_Summ_Nov_2010.pdf

26   Exercising While You're Away With Your Group

You are a youth minister. Your alternate title could be "King of the Road." You've traveled tons of miles and probably stayed in all kinds of hotel rooms, youth camp cabins, and church floors. While it's true that you can't stuff your Soloflex machine into your suitcase, you can get a great workout with little or no equipment available. Don't believe me? Read on...

The 10 Minute Workout for You — the Buff and Mighty Youth Minister

Do all exercises one after the other with little to no rest (if you can. If you need a breather, take it. I'm not watching you)

1. **Standard Push-Ups.** The old reliable. Start with your hands shoulder–width apart and the rest of your body straight. Lower your entire torso to the floor while maintaining a "1-2" count. Push up with your arms while maintaining the same count. If you are a beginner, you can do push-ups with your knees touching the floor instead of your toes. If you are a beginner, do as many as you can without hurting yourself. Everyone else, shoot for 5-10 repetitions.

2. **Squats.** This is a great exercise for your "core" (the midsection of your body) and your legs. Start with a shoulder-width stance. Make sure

that you are looking straight ahead with no bend in your back. Let your arms hang at your side and bend at the knees until you are butt is at (or as close as you can get) the same level as your knees. Slowly straighten your legs until you return to the beginning standing position. Beginners, do what you can. Everyone else, try for 5-10 repetitions.

3. **Single Arm Shoulder Press.** You can do this either seated or standing. Start by holding your right hand up at shoulder level with your palm up, as though you are holding an invisible food servers tray. Place your left hand on top of your right hand and apply a little pressure. Raise your right hand straight up while keeping the left hand on top, applying pressure. Switch arms and repeat the exercise. Beginners, do 5 reps with each arm. Everyone else, shoot for 10-20 repetitions with each arm.

4. **Single Arm Bicep Curl.** In a standing position, let your right arm hang at your side with your palm facing up. Place your left hand on top of your right hand, and apply a little pressure. Pull your right arm up to your shoulder. (You can lock the fingers of both hands together if you wish.) Switch arms and repeat the exercise. Beginners, do 5 reps with each arm. Everyone else, shoot for 10-20 repetitions with each arm.

5. **Jumping Jacks.** Remember these from your P.E. days? Jacks are a great cardio exercise that works all kinds of muscles in your body. Start in a standing position with your hands at your side (palms touching your outer thighs). In one small jumping motion, spread your legs and bring your arms a little higher than shoulder level. Imagine that you are making an "X" with your body. Beginners, try for 10 seconds of consecutive jacks. Everyone else, shoot for 30-60 seconds of continuous jacks.

If you are just starting out, you should begin with one cycle. For those of you that are past the beginning stage of fitness, shoot for 2-4 sets of the 5–exercise cycle. Then take a shower, you will reek.

Bibliography

The Holy Bible. Revised standard version containing the Old and New Testaments. (1952). New York: T. Nelson.

Appreciative inquiry commons. (n.d.). Retrieved from http://appreciativeinquiry.case.edu

Bell, R. (2005). *Velvet Elvis: Repainting the Christian faith.* Grand Rapids, Mich: Zondervan.

Carlin, G. (1997). *Brain droppings.* New York: Hyperion.

Fields, D. (1998). *Purpose-driven youth ministry: 9 essential foundations for healthy growth.* Grand Rapids, Mich: Zondervan

Greene, B. (2006). *The best life diet.* New York: Simon & Schuster.

Harris, A., & Harris, B. (2008). *Do hard things: A teenage rebellion against low expectations.* Colorado Springs, CO: Multnomah Books.

Mayo, J. (2004). *Thriving youth groups: Secrets for growing your ministry.* Loveland, Colo: Group.

Newberry, T. (2007). *The 4:8 principle: The secret to a joy-filled life.* Carol Stream, Ill: Tyndale House Publishers.

Prosperi, W. (2006). *Girls' ministry 101: Ideas for retreats, small groups, and everyday life with teenage girls.* Grand Rapids, Mich: Zondervan.

Schnase, R. C. (2007). *Five practices of fruitful congregations.* Nashville: Abingdon Press.

Twain, M. ( ) *The Adventures of Tom Sawyer*

Warren, R. (2005) *The purpose driven life*. Findaway World Llc.

Wilkinson, B. (2000). *The prayer of Jabez: Breaking through to the blessed life*. Sisters, Or: Multnomah.

Yaconelli, M. (2004). *Mike Yaconelli: Collected writings*. El Cajon, CA: Youth Specialties.

Zinczenko, D., & Spiker, T. (2004). *The abs diet: The six-week plan to flatten your stomach and keep you lean for life*. [Emmaus, Pa.]: Rodale

About the Author

Jay Tucker is a life-long South Floridian. Growing up in Naples, FL gave Jay year-long sun and the foundation for the desire to stay active. This desire pointed him in the direction of education, where he holds a Bachelor Degree from Florida Gulf Coast University. Jay has been married to his wife Kimberly, since 1995. Together they have two beautiful children, Sarah Kay and William Monroe II. After two years in the classroom and a 9/11 shortened stint as a national educational/motivational speaker, Jay finally answered God's call in his life to enter fulltime youth ministry.

That career has spanned 15+ years as both a volunteer and a fulltime salaried employee in the church. Over the years, Jay has attended many youth worker conferences and events. It was during one of those events when Jay made a sobering discovery: a large percentage of his fellow youth workers were extremely overweight. This began a journey into how to help himself and other youth workers achieve and maintain the optimal level of health that will allow us to minister at our full potential.

This book is a humorous look at youth ministry "from the trenches." It is filled with professional tips, spiritual advice, and easy to follow fitness and nutrition tips that are designed to fit naturally into the life of the youth worker. In the future, Jay aspires to help other youth workers find that level of wholeness through his writing and speaking.

For updates on the latest tips and best practices for youth ministry, please visit my new site **www.JayTucker.net**.

Index

www.ingramcontent.com/pod-product-compliance
Lightning Source LLC
Chambersburg PA
CBHW032101080426
42733CB00006B/364